Spicy Black Bean–Corn Casserole,
page 18

Cooking Light.

Slow Cooker

Oxmoor House.

©2006 by Oxmoor House, Inc.
Book Division of Southern Progress Corporation
P.O. Box 2262, Birmingham, Alabama 35201

ISBN-13: 978-0-8487-3068-0
ISBN-10: 0-8487-3068-2
Library of Congress Control Number: 2006929984
Printed in the United States of America
Second printing 2007

Be sure to check with your health-care provider before making any changes in your diet.

Oxmoor House, Inc.
Editor in Chief: Nancy Fitzpatrick Wyatt
Executive Editor: Katherine M. Eakin
Copy Chief: Allison Long Lowery

Cooking Light® Slow Cooker
Editor: Terri Laschober
Food Editor: Anne Cain, M.S., R.D.
Copy Editor: Diane Rose
Editorial Assistant: Julie Boston
Nutrition Editorial Assistant:
    Rachel Quinlivan, R.D.
Photography Director: Jim Bathie
Senior Photo Stylist: Kay E. Clarke
Photo Stylist: Katherine Eckert
Director, Test Kitchens: Elizabeth Tyler Austin
Assistant Director, Test Kitchens:
    Julie Christopher
Test Kitchens Staff: Nicole Lee Faber,
    Kathleen Royal Phillips
Food Stylist: Kelley Self Wilton
Director of Production: Laura Lockhart
Senior Production Manager: Greg A. Amason
Production Assistant: Faye Porter Bonner

Contributors:
Designer: Carol Damsky
Indexer: Mary Ann Laurens
Editorial Interns: Jill Baughman, Ashley Leath,
    Caroline Markunas, Mary Katherine Pappas,
    Vanessa Rusch Thomas, Lucas Whittington
Photographers: Beau Gustafson, Lee Harrelson

To order additional publications, call
1-800-765-6400, or visit **oxmoorhouse.com**

CONTENTS

Essential Slow Cooker 8

Whether it's a big batch of chili for the game, a heartwarming cider, or a pot roast fit for company, some dishes just naturally lend themselves to the slow cooker. Add these beloved *Cooking Light* recipes to your repertoire.

Meats 32

Braising meat in a slow cooker makes for a savory, fork-tender dish every time. For traditional fare, try our meat loaf or beef Burgundy. For more exotic tastes, try the Moroccan-style lamb tagine over couscous.

Poultry 56

Always family favorites, chicken and turkey just got easier with some help from your slow cooker. Serve one of our saucy chicken dishes over rice, and dinner is complete. And we've got a no-fuss turkey recipe that makes an elegant entrée or a satisfying sandwich.

Vegetarian 74

Find hearty meat-free stews and entrées (even a lasagna) that will satisfy the vegetarian appetite. Make a scrumptious filling for burritos. Or bring luck to your table with a bowl of hoppin' John.

Soups & Stews 92

From classic vegetable-beef soup to a Caribbean-inspired seafood lover's feast, these recipes will help you make a filling weeknight meal—and allow for leftovers for lunch the next day.

Sides & Desserts 114

Cook vegetables, steam hearty bread, and concoct delectable sweets. Your slow cooker helps you round out a meal when oven space is scarce.

Cooking Light®
Editor in Chief: Mary Kay Culpepper
Executive Editor: Billy R. Sims
Art Director: Susan Waldrip Dendy
Managing Editor: Maelynn Cheung
Senior Food Editor: Alison Mann Ashton
Features Editor: Phillip Rhodes
Projects Editor: Mary Simpson Creel, M.S., R.D.
Food Editor: Ann Taylor Pittman
Associate Food Editors: Julianna Grimes Bottcher,
    Timothy Q. Cebula
Assistant Food Editor: Kathy C. Kitchens, R.D.
Assistant Editors: Cindy Hatcher,
    Brandy Rushing
Test Kitchens Director: Vanessa Taylor Johnson
Senior Food Stylist: Kellie Gerber Kelley
Food Stylist: M. Kathleen Kanen
Test Kitchens Professionals: Sam Brannock,
    Kathryn Conrad, Mary H. Drennen,
    Jan Jacks Moon, Tiffany Vickers,
    Mike Wilson
Assistant Art Director: Maya Metz Logue
Senior Designers: Fernande Bondarenko,
    J. Shay McNamee
Designer: Brigette Mayer
Senior Photographer: Randy Mayor
Senior Photo Stylist: Cindy Barr
Photo Stylists: Melanie J. Clarke, Jan Gautro
Studio Assistant: Celine Chenoweth
Copy Chief: Maria Parker Hopkins
Senior Copy Editor: Susan Roberts
Copy Editor: Johannah Paiva
Production Manager: Liz Rhoades
Production Editors: Joanne McCrary Brasseal,
    Hazel R. Eddins
Administrative Coordinator: Carol D. Johnson
Office Manager: Rita K. Jackson
Editorial Assistant: Melissa Hoover
Correspondence Editor: Michelle Gibson Daniels
Interns: Sabrina Bone, Kimberly Burnstad,
    Melissa Marek, Molly Kate Matthews,
    Megan Voelkel

CookingLight.com
Editor: Jennifer Middleton Richards
Online Producer: Abigail Masters

Cover: *Osso Buco* (page 46)

Welcome

A slow cooker is versatile, dependable, and just plain convenient. But there's another thing that a slow cooker is, and that's essential. For a *Cooking Light*® cook, a slow cooker makes it easier to cook healthy, delicious food and still have time left over to enjoy the day.

In this cookbook, you'll find the slow-cooker recipes we believe to be essential for every *Cooking Light* cook. These recipes are tried-and-true classics—ones we love to make again and again.

Each chapter offers mouthwatering, flavorful recipes, complete with nutritional analyses that will help you eat smart, be fit, and live well.

So whether you're looking for a humble recipe for Beef and Bean Chili or for something with the finesse of Osso Buco, you're sure to find it in this edition of *The Cooking Light Cook's Essential Recipe Collection*.

Very truly yours,

Mary Kay Culpepper
Editor in Chief

essential
slow cooker

Overnight Apple Butter

1 cup packed brown sugar
½ cup honey
¼ cup apple cider
1 tablespoon ground cinnamon
¼ teaspoon ground cloves
⅛ teaspoon ground mace
10 apples, peeled, cored, and cut into large chunks (about 2½ pounds)

1. Combine all ingredients in a 5-quart electric slow cooker. Cover and cook on LOW 10 hours or until apples are very tender.

2. Place a large fine-mesh sieve over a bowl; spoon one-third of apple mixture into sieve. Press mixture through sieve using the back of a spoon or ladle. Discard pulp. Repeat procedure with remaining apple mixture. Return apple mixture to cooker. Cook, uncovered, on HIGH 1½ hours or until mixture is thick, stirring occasionally. Spoon into a bowl; cover and chill up to 1 week. Yield: 4 cups (serving size: ¼ cup).

CALORIES 132 (0% from fat); FAT 0g; PROTEIN 0.1g; CARB 35.3g; FIBER 3.1g; CHOL 0mg; IRON 0.7mg; SODIUM 6mg; CALC 18mg

A mixture of apple varieties, rather than just one type, will produce apple butter with a rich, complex flavor. Balancing a tart apple, such as a Granny Smith (shown right), with a sweeter variety, such as a Rome (shown left), will make for an ideal combination. Other good choices include sweet Jonathan, Stayman, and York apples mixed with tart Northern Spy or Winesap varieties. Whatever combination you choose, look for firm, vibrantly colored apples that smell fresh and don't have bruises. A good apple from a roadside stand or farmers' market will always translate to premium flavor and texture.

Your home will be filled with sweet aromas as cinnamon, cloves, and mace infuse rich, earthy apples. Enjoy the apple butter over toast or English muffins as a healthy alternative to real butter, or serve it as a condiment with pork chops or chicken. This apple butter also makes a terrific gift. Just divide it into jars and label each one with a tag telling recipients to keep it in the refrigerator.

Maple-Hazelnut Oatmeal

1½ cups fat-free milk
1½ cups water
  2 Gala apples, peeled, cored, and cut into ½-inch cubes (about 3 cups)
  1 cup uncooked steel-cut oats
  2 tablespoons brown sugar
1½ tablespoons butter, softened
  ¼ teaspoon ground cinnamon
  ¼ teaspoon salt
Cooking spray
  ¼ cup pure maple syrup
  2 tablespoons chopped hazelnuts, toasted

1. Bring milk and water to a boil in a saucepan over medium-high heat, stirring frequently.

2. Place hot milk mixture, apple, and next 5 ingredients in a 3-quart electric slow cooker coated with cooking spray; stir well. Cover and cook on LOW 7 hours or until oats are tender.

3. Ladle oatmeal into individual bowls; top with maple syrup and hazelnuts. Yield: 4 servings (serving size: 1¼ cups oatmeal, 1 tablespoon syrup, and 1½ teaspoons hazelnuts).

CALORIES 341 (24% from fat); FAT 9.2g (sat 3.4g, mono 2.8g, poly 0.5g); PROTEIN 9.9g; CARB 60.6g; FIBER 5.5g; CHOL 13mg; IRON 2.4mg; SODIUM 218mg; CALC 163mg

Steel-cut oats (also called Irish oatmeal) are cracked whole-grain oats that have a chewy texture when cooked. Unlike more widely available rolled oats, steel-cut oats are not steamed and flattened. As a result, they take longer to cook, making them an ideal fit for the slow cooker. These oats are wonderfully hearty and are a good source of iron as well as both soluble and insoluble fiber.

Cooked with apples and cinnamon and topped with maple syrup and hazelnuts, this oatmeal is anything but ordinary. This high-fiber breakfast will satisfy your hunger, provide long-lasting energy, and help your mind stay focused.

Hot Mulled Ginger-Spiced Cider

3 whole cloves
2 (4 x 1–inch) strips orange rind
2 whole allspice
1 (3-inch) cinnamon stick
1 (½-inch) piece peeled fresh ginger
12 cups apple cider
½ cup apple jelly
¼ teaspoon ground nutmeg

1. Place first 5 ingredients on a 5-inch-square double layer of cheesecloth. Gather edges of cheesecloth together, and tie securely.

2. Place cheesecloth bag, cider, jelly, and ground nutmeg in a 4½-quart electric slow cooker. Cover and cook on HIGH 4 hours. Remove and discard cheesecloth bag. Yield: 12 servings (serving size: 1 cup).

CALORIES 174 (0% from fat); FAT 0g; PROTEIN 1g; CARB 43.8g; FIBER 0g; CHOL 0mg; IRON 0mg; SODIUM 0mg; CALC 0mg

Cloves, orange rind, allspice, cinnamon, and ginger infuse this cider with their soothing aromas and flavors. But no one enjoys fishing stray cloves out of his or her mug. A simple spice bag made from cheesecloth and kitchen twine allows for easy removal of the spices and rind when the cider's done.

This cider will fill your home and spirit with holiday cheer. When it's ready, turn the slow cooker to LOW to keep the cider warm, and have guests help themselves. You can dress up the presentation by adding cinnamon sticks or orange rind strips to individual servings.

Cheesy Spinach-Artichoke Dip

Feta, a semifirm cheese that's sold either crumbled or in a block packed in brine, lends its distinctive salty, tangy flavor to this dip. Dairy products like feta, cream cheese, and sour cream tend to break down when cooked for extended periods of time in the slow cooker, but they hold up well in this dip because it's only cooked for a couple of hours on LOW.

11 (6-inch) pitas
1/3 cup chopped sun-dried
   tomatoes, packed without oil
1 cup boiling water
1 (14-ounce) can quartered
   artichoke hearts, drained
   and coarsely chopped
1 (10-ounce) package frozen
   chopped spinach, thawed,
   drained, and squeezed dry
1 (8-ounce) tub light cream
   cheese, softened
1 (8-ounce) carton reduced-fat
   sour cream
3/4 cup grated Parmesan cheese
3/4 cup fat-free milk
1/2 cup (2 ounces) crumbled
   reduced-fat feta cheese
1/2 cup diced onion
1/2 cup fat-free mayonnaise
1 tablespoon red wine vinegar
1/4 teaspoon freshly ground
   black pepper
2 garlic cloves, crushed

1. Preheat oven to 350°.
2. Split each pita in half horizontally; cut each half into 6 wedges. Place pita wedges in a single layer on baking sheets; bake at 350° for 10 minutes or until toasted.
3. Combine sun-dried tomatoes and boiling water in a bowl; let stand 1 hour or until soft.
4. Place artichokes and next 11 ingredients in a 3-quart electric slow cooker; stir well. Cover and cook on LOW 1 hour. Drain tomatoes, and stir into dip. Cover and cook 1 hour. Serve warm with toasted pita wedges. Yield: 5 1/4 cups dip (serving size: 1/4 cup dip and 6 pita wedges).

CALORIES 162 (25% from fat); FAT 4.5g (sat 2.8g, mono 0.3g, poly 0.1g); PROTEIN 8.1g; CARB 22.3g; FIBER 1.3g; CHOL 15mg; IRON 2mg; SODIUM 329mg; CALC 126mg

Guests will be delighted to find this restaurant favorite on your buffet table. Get this appetizer started in the slow cooker a couple of hours ahead, and then make your final party preparations. The dip will be ready just as partygoers begin to arrive. If you prefer, buy pre-baked pita chips to save time.

Spicy Black Bean–Corn Casserole

Dry corn muffin mix, which contains cornmeal, flour, leavening, and salt, is the short-cut ingredient in this casserole's crust. Don't confuse corn bread or muffin mix with self-rising cornmeal, which contains only cornmeal, leavening, and salt. The mix requires only a liquid, in this case egg substitute, to make corn bread. Green chiles add heat to the batter to balance out the corn muffin mix's sweetness.

3 tablespoons diced green chiles, divided
½ cup salsa
¼ cup chopped green onions
¼ cup chopped fresh cilantro
1 (15-ounce) can black beans, rinsed and drained
1 (11-ounce) can corn with red and green bell peppers, drained
1 (10-ounce) can enchilada sauce
½ cup egg substitute
1 (8½-ounce) package corn muffin mix
2 tablespoons chopped bottled roasted red bell peppers
1½ cups (6 ounces) preshredded reduced-fat Mexican blend or Cheddar cheese
6 tablespoons reduced-fat sour cream
1½ teaspoons thinly sliced fresh cilantro

1. Place 2 tablespoons green chiles and next 6 ingredients in a 3½-quart electric slow cooker; stir well. Cover and cook on LOW 4 hours.

2. Combine remaining 1 tablespoon green chiles, egg substitute, muffin mix, and roasted red bell peppers in a bowl. Spoon batter evenly over bean mixture in cooker. Cover and cook 1 hour or until corn bread is done.

3. Sprinkle cheese over corn bread. Cover and cook 5 minutes or until cheese melts. Top each serving with sour cream; sprinkle with cilantro. Yield: 6 servings (serving size: about 1 cup casserole, 1 tablespoon sour cream, and ¼ teaspoon cilantro).

CALORIES 366 (30% from fat); FAT 12.4g (sat 5.8g, mono 0g, poly 0.1g); PROTEIN 17.2g; CARB 49.6g; FIBER 5.6g; CHOL 28mg; IRON 2.7mg; SODIUM 1,407mg; CALC 307mg

This spicy vegetarian entrée has all the flavors of enchiladas, but instead of using it to fill corn tortillas, you top the saucy black bean and corn mixture with a corn bread batter just before the last hour of cooking. For a complete meal, serve with a salad of mixed greens, orange sections, and sliced avocado dressed in a light vinaigrette.

Company Pot Roast

Vegetables such as carrots, onions, and potatoes cook more slowly than meats, so layer your veggies in the slow cooker before you add the meat. This allows them to have direct contact with the bottom and sides of the cooker, helping them to cook faster.

1 (2-pound) boneless chuck roast, trimmed and cut in half
¼ cup low-sodium soy sauce
2 garlic cloves, minced
1 cup beef broth
1 (.35-ounce) package dried morels or dried shiitake mushrooms
1 tablespoon cracked black pepper
3 tablespoons sun-dried tomato paste or regular tomato paste
2 medium onions (about ¾ pound), quartered
1 (16-ounce) package carrots, cut into 2-inch pieces
16 small red potatoes (about 2 pounds), halved
1 tablespoon canola oil
1½ tablespoons all-purpose flour
3 tablespoons water

1. Combine roast, soy sauce, and garlic in a large zip-top plastic bag; seal bag, and marinate in refrigerator at least 8 hours, turning bag occasionally.

2. Bring broth to a boil in a small saucepan; add mushrooms. Remove from heat; cover and let stand 20 minutes. Drain mushrooms through a cheesecloth-lined colander over a bowl, reserving broth mixture.

3. Remove roast from bag, reserving marinade. Sprinkle roast with pepper, gently pressing pepper into roast. Combine reserved marinade, mushroom broth mixture, and tomato paste; stir well, and set aside.

4. Place mushrooms, onion, carrot, and potato in a 6-quart electric slow cooker; toss gently.

5. Heat oil in a large skillet over medium-high heat, and add roast, browning well on all sides. Place roast over vegetables in cooker. Pour tomato paste mixture into pan, scraping to loosen browned bits. Pour tomato paste mixture over roast and vegetables. Cover and cook on LOW 10 hours or until roast is tender. Place roast and vegetables on a serving platter; keep warm. Reserve cooking liquid in cooker; increase heat to HIGH.

6. Place flour in a bowl. Gradually add water, stirring with a whisk until well blended. Add flour mixture to cooking liquid in cooker. Cook, uncovered, 15 minutes or until slightly thick, stirring frequently. Serve gravy with roast and vegetables. Yield: 8 servings (serving size: 3 ounces roast, 1 onion wedge, about 3 carrot pieces, 4 potato halves, and about ¼ cup gravy).

CALORIES 358 (33% from fat); FAT 13.2g (sat 3.7g, mono 5.3g, poly 1.1g); PROTEIN 27g; CARB 32.1g; FIBER 4.9g; CHOL 69mg; IRON 4.4mg; SODIUM 746mg; CALC 52mg

Though this delicious meal takes some planning ahead, you'll be glad when you can spend the time before dinner chatting with family and friends instead of busily running around the kitchen. Use leftover meat and gravy to make great roast beef sandwiches the next day.

Knife-and-Fork Barbecued Brisket Sandwiches

Brown sugar, a common ingredient in barbecue sauce, owes its moist, soft texture and caramel-like flavor to molasses (a small amount of which is added to granulated sugar to create brown sugar). For this recipe, use light brown sugar for a delicate molasses flavor. Dark brown sugar contains more molasses and adds a bolder, more toffeelike flavor to recipes. Just two tablespoons of brown sugar, along with the beer, will temper the heat of the chili sauce and horseradish, yielding a well-balanced sauce.

1 (3-pound) beef brisket, trimmed
2 tablespoons all-purpose flour
2 large onions, thinly sliced and divided
1 teaspoon black pepper
¼ teaspoon salt
1 (12-ounce) bottle chili sauce
½ cup light beer
2 tablespoons brown sugar
1 tablespoon prepared horseradish
4 large garlic cloves, minced, or 1 tablespoon bottled minced garlic
12 (1-ounce) slices barbecue bread with sesame seeds, toasted

1. Cut brisket into 4 pieces. Dredge pieces in flour, reserving any remaining flour.

2. Place half of onion in a 4-quart electric slow cooker, and top with beef. Sprinkle with reserved flour, pepper, and salt. Arrange remaining half of onion over beef.

3. Combine chili sauce and next 4 ingredients; stir well. Pour over beef mixture. Cover and cook on HIGH 1 hour. Reduce heat to LOW, and cook 7 to 8 hours or until beef is tender. Remove beef with a slotted spoon. Replace cooker lid.

4. Shred beef with 2 forks; return beef to cooker, stirring well. Spoon beef mixture over toasted bread. Yield: 12 servings (serving size: ¾ cup beef mixture and 1 slice toast).

CALORIES 271 (18% from fat); FAT 5.4g (sat 1.6g, mono 1.8g, poly 0.7g); PROTEIN 27.9g; CARB 27.5g; FIBER 1.5g; CHOL 46mg; IRON 3.1mg; SODIUM 1,009mg; CALC 49mg

Sink your teeth into melt-in-your mouth barbecue without the hassle of a fire pit. Beef brisket lends itself perfectly to the slow cooker, since long, slow, moist heat is the key to transforming this cut into succulent, tender barbecue. Onions add flavor to the meat and caramelize in the process, offering a nice addition to the sandwiches. A thick piece of toasted bread makes a fitting bed for the beef and its flavorful juices. Pair with a refreshing cucumber salad, break out the knife and fork, and dig in.

Beef and Bean Chili

Browning the ground beef before adding it to the slow cooker allows the beef to take on a more appealing color, and you can drain off any grease that accumulates in the pan. Plus, the chili can cook for the entire time on LOW (in order to reach a safe temperature quickly enough, raw meat needs to cook for 1 hour on HIGH before cooking on LOW).

1 pound ground round
1 cup chopped onion
½ cup chopped green bell pepper
¼ cup dry red wine or water
1 tablespoon chili powder
1 teaspoon sugar
1 teaspoon ground cumin
¼ teaspoon salt
1 garlic clove, minced
1 (15-ounce) can kidney beans, undrained
1 (14.5-ounce) can Mexican-style stewed tomatoes with jalapeño peppers and spices, undrained

1. Cook ground round in a large nonstick skillet over medium-high heat until brown, stirring to crumble. Add onion and next 7 ingredients, and cook 7 minutes or until onion is tender. Place meat mixture in a 4-quart electric slow cooker; stir in beans and tomatoes. Cover and cook on LOW 4 hours. Yield: 6 servings (serving size: 1¼ cups).

CALORIES 233 (30% from fat); FAT 7.7g (sat 3.1g, mono 3.3g, poly 0.3g); PROTEIN 20.6g; CARB 20.5g; FIBER 5.2g; CHOL 49mg; IRON 3.2mg; SODIUM 597mg; CALC 65mg

Your family will love this soul-warming chili. Increase the amount of chili powder or top servings with pickled jalapeño peppers if you prefer spicier food. Serve with crackers, or try our corn bread recipe on page 141. You can double this chili recipe for a crowd, but make sure to use an appropriately sized slow cooker—your cooker should be between half and two-thirds full.

Pork Chops and Gravy

1 tablespoon canola oil,
  divided
6 (6-ounce) bone-in center-cut
  loin pork chops (about ½
  inch thick), trimmed
1 (14-ounce) can fat-free,
  less-sodium chicken broth
1½ teaspoons dry mustard
¾ teaspoon salt
½ teaspoon garlic powder
⅔ cup all-purpose flour
3 cups hot cooked mashed
  potatoes
Freshly ground black pepper
  (optional)

1. Heat 1½ teaspoons oil in a large skillet over medium-high heat. Add 3 chops; cook 2 minutes on each side or until browned. Place chops in a 4½-quart electric slow cooker. Repeat procedure with remaining oil and chops.
2. Combine broth, mustard, salt, and garlic powder. Pour broth mixture over chops in cooker. Cover and cook on LOW 6 hours or until chops are tender. Remove chops from cooker, reserving cooking liquid. Keep chops warm. Increase heat to HIGH.
3. Lightly spoon flour into dry measuring cups; level with a knife. Combine flour and 1 cup cooking liquid, stirring with a whisk until well blended. Stir flour mixture into cooking liquid in cooker. Cook, uncovered, 10 minutes or until thick, stirring occasionally. Serve gravy over chops and potatoes. Sprinkle with pepper, if desired. Yield: 6 servings (serving size: 1 chop, about ⅓ cup gravy, and ½ cup potatoes).

CALORIES 325 (26% from fat); FAT 9.5g (sat 2.7g, mono 4.5g, poly 1.2g); PROTEIN 29.6g; CARB 26.2g; FIBER 3.4g; CHOL 69mg; IRON 1.7mg; SODIUM 554mg; CALC 30mg

One trick to thicken the juices that accumulate in your slow cooker is to make a slurry. Simply whisk together flour and a liquid (water, milk, or some of the cooking liquid), and add it to the juices in the cooker. Cook on HIGH, uncovered, until the liquid thickens, stirring occasionally. Here, this method makes a flavorful gravy for pork chops.

Use our recipe for mashed potatoes on page 141 to accompany these stick-to-your-ribs pork chops. Or purchase a package of refrigerated mashed potatoes (such as Simply Potatoes), and cook them in the microwave according to the package directions. Fresh steamed green beans complete the healthy meal.

Provençale Chicken Supper

4 chicken breast halves (about
  1½ pounds), skinned
2 teaspoons dried basil
¼ teaspoon salt, divided
¼ teaspoon black pepper,
  divided
1 cup diced yellow bell
  pepper
1 (16-ounce) can navy beans,
  rinsed and drained
1 (14½-ounce) can pasta-style
  tomatoes, undrained
Basil leaves (optional)

1. Place chicken in a 4½-quart electric slow cooker; sprinkle with dried basil, ⅛ teaspoon salt, and ⅛ teaspoon black pepper.

2. Combine remaining ⅛ teaspoon salt, remaining ⅛ teaspoon black pepper, bell pepper, beans, and tomatoes in a bowl; stir well. Spoon over chicken. Cover and cook on HIGH 1 hour. Reduce heat to LOW, and cook 5 hours. Spoon bean mixture into 4 shallow bowls; top each with 1 chicken breast half. Garnish with basil leaves, if desired. Yield: 4 servings (serving size: 1 chicken breast half and about ¾ cup bean mixture).

CALORIES 253 (6% from fat); FAT 1.8g (sat 0.5g, mono 0.4g, poly 0.5g); PROTEIN 32.4g; CARB 26.8g; FIBER 6g; CHOL 64mg; IRON 3mg; SODIUM 866mg; CALC 82mg

Both sweet and hot peppers were introduced to Europe by Christopher Columbus, who brought these members of the *Capsicum* family back from the New World. Bell peppers are available in green, yellow, orange, red, purple, and brown. Color depends on variety and ripeness. When they're picked before maturity, they are green; when they're left on the vine, they change color. Because yellow, red, and orange bell peppers stay on the vine longer and are more perishable than green, they cost more. For the freshest bell peppers, look for brightly colored, glossy skins that are free of spots and wrinkles.

This rustic dish takes its cue from the typical fare served in Provence, a region in the southeastern part of France that is known for dishes highlighting fresh local ingredients such as garlic, tomatoes, olive oil, olives, and sweet bell peppers. Be sure to use bone-in chicken breasts for this recipe, or substitute bone-in chicken thighs. For a hearty weeknight meal, serve this dish with crusty bread to soak up the juices.

Fudgy Caramel Pudding Cake

1 (19.8-ounce) package fudge
    brownie mix
1 cup water
½ cup applesauce
3 tablespoons canola oil
1 large egg
1 large egg white
Cooking spray
½ cup fat-free caramel sundae
    syrup
2 tablespoons chopped
    walnuts or pecans
3 cups water
2¾ cups vanilla fat-free frozen
    yogurt

A pan or soufflé dish and a little water can turn your slow cooker into a small oven that's ideal for baking breads and cakes with steam heat. Make sure your dish fits inside the cooker before you start. Try our Steamed Brown Bread with Currants and Walnuts (recipe on page 126) for another recipe that uses this method.

1. Combine first 5 ingredients in a large bowl; stir 50 strokes with a wooden spoon. Set aside.
2. Beat egg white with a mixer at high speed until stiff peaks form. Gently fold egg white into batter. Pour batter into a 2-quart soufflé dish or deep-sided round baking dish coated with cooking spray. Drizzle caramel syrup over batter; sprinkle with nuts (caramel will sink to bottom).
3. Place a long sheet of foil over top of dish; wrap edges under dish. Place dish on top of another long sheet of foil; press foil against sides and over top of dish, completely enclosing dish. Place a small rack, trivet, or 3 canning jar rings in a round 5-quart electric slow cooker; pour 3 cups water into cooker. Place dish on rack. Cover and cook on HIGH 4½ hours or until pudding is set. Remove dish from cooker using oven mitts, and remove foil; let pudding stand 20 minutes. Spoon into parfait glasses or dessert bowls; top with frozen yogurt. Yield: 11 servings (serving size: ½ cup pudding cake and ¼ cup frozen yogurt).

CALORIES 378 (27% from fat); FAT 11.3g (sat 1.8g, mono 5.6g, poly 2.1g); PROTEIN 5.7g; CARB 63.1g; FIBER 0.3g; CHOL 19mg; IRON 1.9mg; SODIUM 240mg; CALC 53mg

Cake in the slow cooker? You won't believe how simple it is to create moist, decadent desserts in this hands-off appliance. Making dessert in the slow cooker can save the oven for the main course, and it gives you a make-ahead option for an otherwise time-consuming dish. When serving this dessert, be sure to scoop all the way to the bottom of the dish to get the warm caramel sauce.

meats

Corned Beef and Vegetables

When cutting a cabbage into wedges, it is important to keep part of its core intact to keep the wedges together. To do this, place the cabbage on a cutting board with its stem down. Make one cut lengthwise down the center. Cut each half, working from the core and angling outward, into five equal wedges. Adding the cabbage wedges during the last hour of cooking will ensure they maintain some of their texture.

20 small boiling onions (about 1 pound), peeled
10 medium carrots (about 1¾ pounds), peeled and quartered
10 small red potatoes (about 1¼ pounds)
2 bay leaves
1 (3¾-pound) cured corned beef brisket with spice packet, trimmed and cut in half
1 (12-ounce) bottle amber beer
½ cup Dijon mustard, divided
3 tablespoons molasses
2 large garlic cloves, crushed
1 small cabbage, cut into 10 wedges (about 1½ pounds)

1. Place first 4 ingredients in a 6½-quart electric slow cooker. Reserve spice packet from brisket; place brisket on top of vegetables.
2. Combine reserved spice packet, beer, 3 tablespoons mustard, molasses, and garlic in a bowl; stir well with a whisk. Pour mixture over brisket. Cover and cook on HIGH 1 hour. Reduce heat to LOW, and cook 6 hours. Add cabbage; cover and cook 1 hour or until tender. Discard bay leaves.
3. Cut brisket across grain into thin slices. Serve corned beef and vegetables with remaining 5 tablespoons mustard. Yield: 10 servings (serving size: about 3 ounces brisket, 2 onions, 4 carrot pieces, 1 potato, 1 cabbage wedge, and 1½ teaspoons mustard).

CALORIES 340 (44% from fat); FAT 16.5g (sat 5.5g, mono 7.9g, poly 0.7g); PROTEIN 18.5g; CARB 28.8g; FIBER 4.8g; CHOL 83mg; IRON 2.9mg; SODIUM 1,188mg; CALC 84mg

Rich amber beer, Dijon mustard, and molasses infuse corned beef and its favorite partners—potatoes, cabbage, and carrots—for a palate-pleasing balance of flavors. Corned beef is a brisket cut that's been cured or "corned" in a brine that's usually seasoned with peppercorns and bay leaves. Sometimes corned beef comes with a spice packet. If you can't find one that does, add 1 teaspoon black peppercorns to the cooking liquid.

Beef Daube Provençal

When cubing meat for a stew, cut the pieces to a uniform size to ensure even cooking. Otherwise, smaller pieces of meat will cook too quickly and become over-done, while the larger pieces will need to cook longer. Begin by trimming any visible fat; then cut the roast into 2-inch-thick slices. Cut slices into 2-inch cubes.

2 teaspoons olive oil
12 garlic cloves, crushed
1 (2-pound) boneless chuck roast, trimmed and cut into 2-inch cubes
1½ teaspoons salt, divided
½ teaspoon freshly ground black pepper, divided
1 cup red wine
2 cups chopped carrot
1½ cups chopped onion
½ cup less-sodium beef broth
1 tablespoon tomato paste
1 teaspoon chopped fresh rosemary
1 teaspoon chopped fresh thyme
Dash of ground cloves
1 (14.5-ounce) can diced tomatoes, undrained
1 bay leaf
3 cups hot cooked medium egg noodles (about 4 cups uncooked pasta)

1. Preheat oven to 300°.

2. Heat oil in a small Dutch oven over low heat. Add garlic, and cook 5 minutes or until garlic is fragrant, stirring occasionally. Remove garlic with a slotted spoon, and set aside. Increase heat to medium-high. Add roast to pan; sprinkle with ½ teaspoon salt and ¼ teaspoon pepper. Cook 5 minutes, browning on all sides. Remove roast from pan. Add wine to pan; bring to a boil, scraping pan to loosen browned bits. Add garlic, roast, remaining 1 teaspoon salt, remaining ¼ teaspoon pepper, carrot, and next 8 ingredients. Bring to a boil.

3. Place roast mixture in a 4-quart electric slow cooker. Cover and cook on HIGH 5 hours. Discard bay leaf. Serve over noodles. Yield: 6 servings (serving size: about ¾ cup stew and ½ cup noodles).

Note: To make in an oven, prepare through Step 2. Cover Dutch oven, and bake at 300° for 2½ hours or until beef is tender.

CALORIES 367 (31% from fat); FAT 12.8g (sat 4.3g, mono 5.8g, poly 0.9g); PROTEIN 29.1g; CARB 33.4g; FIBER 3.9g; CHOL 105mg; IRON 4.3mg; SODIUM 776mg; CALC 76mg

This classic French stew made with braised beef, red wine, and vegetables is simple and delicious. It's perfect cold-weather fare, and it's versatile, too. Serve alone for an easy weeknight meal, or try it with a whole-grain baguette and a mixed green salad tossed with bottled vinaigrette for special occasions. Mashed potatoes are a good substitute for the noodles; try our recipe for mashed potatoes on page 141.

Beef Burgundy

Pearl onions, also known as pickling onions, are small and mild in flavor. To peel them easily, slice off their root ends, and drop them into boiling water for 1 minute. Drain and rinse with cold water. Pinch the stem end of each, and a peeled onion will pop out. Substitute 1 (16-ounce) bag frozen small whole onions, thawed and drained, for the fresh onions in this recipe, if desired.

1 (10-ounce) package fresh pearl onions
1 (2-pound) top round steak, trimmed and cut into 1½-inch cubes
2½ cups sliced onion (1 large)
1 garlic clove, minced
Cooking spray
⅓ cup all-purpose flour
1⅓ cups less-sodium beef broth
½ cup Burgundy or other dry red wine
2 tablespoons tomato paste
½ teaspoon dried thyme
½ teaspoon salt
¼ teaspoon black pepper
1 bay leaf
1 (8-ounce) package mushrooms
3 cups hot cooked medium egg noodles (about 4 cups uncooked pasta)
Thyme leaves (optional)

1. Drop pearl onions in boiling water; cook 1 minute. Drain onions; peel.
2. Heat a large nonstick skillet over medium-high heat. Add steak; sauté 5 minutes or until browned. Place steak in a 3-quart electric slow cooker. Add sliced onion and garlic to pan; coat with cooking spray, and sauté over medium-high heat 5 minutes or until tender. Lightly spoon flour into a dry measuring cup; level with a knife. Sprinkle flour over onion-garlic mixture; cook 1 minute, stirring constantly. Gradually add broth, wine, and tomato paste, stirring constantly. Cook 1 minute or until thick. Add pearl onions, dried thyme, salt, pepper, bay leaf, and mushrooms.
3. Pour wine mixture over steak in cooker. Cover and cook on LOW 6 to 7 hours. Discard bay leaf. Serve over noodles. Garnish with thyme leaves, if desired. Yield: 6 servings (serving size: 1 cup steak mixture and ½ cup noodles).

CALORIES 398 (18% from fat); FAT 8.1g (sat 2.5g, mono 3.1g, poly 0.8g); PROTEIN 41.7g; CARB 38.1g; FIBER 3.3g; CHOL 106mg; IRON 5.1mg; SODIUM 392mg; CALC 67mg

Beef Burgundy (or boeuf bourguignon in French) is a rich beef stew flavored with, as the name suggests, Burgundy wine. It's often served as a sauce over egg noodles. A traditional version of this dish can take hours of work tending to various steps on the cooktop and in the oven. This slow-cooker version has the flavor of all-day cooking without making you spend your entire day watching over it. Serve with a mixed green salad for a complete meal.

Beef Stroganoff

Sour cream is the key component to a good beef stroganoff's rich sauce. Be sure to take the time to let the dish stand uncovered for 10 minutes with the cooker off before stirring in the sour cream. If sour cream is heated too long or at too high of a temperature, it will break down and begin to curdle.

1 (1-pound) top round steak (1 inch thick), trimmed
1 cup chopped onion
2 tablespoons chopped fresh parsley
2 tablespoons Dijon mustard
¾ teaspoon salt
½ teaspoon dried dill
½ teaspoon black pepper
1 (8-ounce) package presliced mushrooms (about 2 cups)
3 garlic cloves, minced
⅓ cup all-purpose flour
1 cup less-sodium beef broth
1 (8-ounce) container reduced-fat sour cream
2 cups hot cooked medium egg noodles (about 1½ cups uncooked pasta)
Chopped fresh dill (optional)

1. Cut steak diagonally across grain into ¾-inch-thick slices. Place steak and next 8 ingredients in a 3-quart electric slow cooker; stir well.

2. Lightly spoon flour into a dry measuring cup, and level with a knife. Place flour in a small bowl, and gradually add broth, stirring with a whisk until blended. Add broth mixture to cooker, and stir well. Cover and cook on HIGH 1 hour. Reduce heat to LOW, and cook 7 to 8 hours or until steak is tender. Turn cooker off; remove lid. Let stroganoff stand 10 minutes. Stir in sour cream. Serve stroganoff over noodles. Sprinkle with chopped dill, if desired. Yield: 4 servings (serving size: about 1 cup stroganoff and ½ cup noodles).

CALORIES 444 (32% from fat); FAT 15.9g (sat 7.4g, mono 3.4g, poly 0.9g); PROTEIN 35.7g; CARB 38.8g; FIBER 2.6g; CHOL 123mg; IRON 4.7mg; SODIUM 737mg; CALC 123mg

The slow cooker helps make this classic dish a weeknight supper your family will love. You may have most of the ingredients on hand in your pantry, and with minimal prep time, you can have this cooking before you leave for the day. When you're ready to eat, boil the egg noodles while the stroganoff stands, and everything will be ready to serve at the same time. A side of broccoli or Brussels sprouts will complement this satisfying pasta dish quite nicely.

Meat Loaf with Shiitake Mushrooms

Originally from Asia, shiitake mushrooms lend themselves to a variety of cooking styles. Dried shiitakes, which are more chewy in texture and have a more intense flavor, are available, but make sure to use fresh mushrooms in this recipe. Fresh shiitakes contribute a meaty texture and moisture to the meat loaf, allowing for leaner ground meats to be used. When buying fresh shiitakes, look for plump mushrooms with edges that curl under. The stems should be tender enough to chop with the caps, but if you feel resistance from your knife, discard the stems.

2 (1-ounce) slices whole wheat bread
¾ pound ground round
¾ pound ground turkey
1½ cups coarsely chopped shiitake mushrooms
½ cup grated fresh onion
1 teaspoon dried Italian seasoning
¾ teaspoon salt
2 large eggs, lightly beaten
1 garlic clove, minced
2 tablespoons ketchup
1½ teaspoons Dijon mustard
⅛ teaspoon ground red pepper

1. Place bread in a food processor, and pulse 10 times or until crumbs measure 1⅓ cups. Combine crumbs, beef, and next 7 ingredients in a large bowl, and shape beef mixture into a 9 x 6–inch loaf. Place loaf in a 3-quart oval electric slow cooker.

2. Combine ketchup, mustard, and pepper in a small bowl, stirring with a fork. Spread ketchup mixture evenly over top of loaf. Cover and cook on HIGH 1 hour. Reduce heat to LOW, and cook 3 hours. Yield: 6 servings (serving size: 4 ounces).

CALORIES 265 (43% from fat); FAT 12.7g (sat 4.2g, mono 5.1g, poly 1.7g); PROTEIN 25.2g; CARB 12.7g; FIBER 1.9g; CHOL 152mg; IRON 3mg; SODIUM 545mg; CALC 41mg

Traditional meat loaf gets a quick and healthy face-lift with lean ground meat, shiitake mushrooms, and hands-off cooking in the slow cooker. The cooker's lid prevents any moisture from escaping from the cooker, resulting in an especially moist and tender meat loaf. Serve with steamed green beans and mashed potatoes for dinner tonight, and save the leftovers for sandwiches.

Picadillo

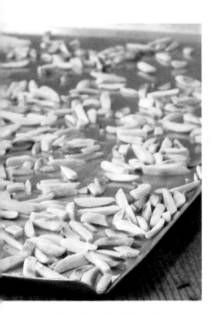

Toasting the slivered almonds before stirring them into the pot gives a richer, more nutty taste to this lively Latin dish. Spread the almonds on a baking sheet, and bake at 350° for 6 to 8 minutes. Or place the almonds in a dry skillet, and cook over medium heat, stirring frequently, for 1 to 2 minutes or until they're toasted. Be sure to watch them carefully; they can go from toasted to burned very quickly.

2 pounds ground round
1½ cups chopped green bell pepper
1 cup chopped onion
1 cup sliced green onions
4 garlic cloves, minced
1 (14½-ounce) can diced tomatoes, undrained
1 (8-ounce) can tomato sauce
⅓ cup chopped pitted dates
⅓ cup chopped dried apricots
¼ cup sliced pimiento-stuffed olives
1 tablespoon ground cumin
1 teaspoon ground cinnamon
½ teaspoon salt
½ teaspoon dried oregano
¼ teaspoon ground red pepper
¼ teaspoon black pepper
¼ cup slivered almonds, toasted
4½ cups hot cooked rice

1. Cook beef, bell pepper, onion, green onions, and garlic in a large nonstick skillet over medium-high heat until beef is browned, stirring to crumble beef. Drain well.
2. Place beef mixture in a 4-quart electric slow cooker. Add diced tomatoes and next 10 ingredients; stir well. Cover and cook on HIGH 3 hours. Stir in almonds. Serve over rice. Yield: 9 servings (serving size: ¾ cup picadillo and ½ cup rice).

CALORIES 391 (29% from fat); FAT 12.5g (sat 4.3g, mono 5.7g, poly 0.8g); PROTEIN 24.7g; CARB 44.2g; FIBER 4.1g; CHOL 66mg; IRON 4.8mg; SODIUM 482mg; CALC 67mg

Picadillo is a favorite dish in many Spanish-speaking countries. It always starts with a ground pork, beef, or veal base that is mixed with various ingredients that provide the dish's signature sweet and savory flavors. In this version, sweet dates and dried apricots mingle with smoky cumin, spicy ground red pepper, and salty olives for a union of interesting flavors. In Mexican cooking, picadillo is often served with flour tortillas. Cubans enjoy it over rice with black beans and fried plantains. Either way, our slow-cooker version makes a festive meal that family and friends will enjoy.

Osso Buco

Before chopping fresh rosemary, you must first remove the leaves from the tough, woody stem. Working over a cutting board, hold the top of your rosemary sprig with the leaves pointing toward you. With your other hand, run your fingers along the stem against the direction of the leaves, pinching tightly. Your fingers will separate the leaves from the stem. Mound the leaves together on your cutting board, and then chop the leaves with a chef's knife.

2 tablespoons all-purpose
   flour
¾ teaspoon black pepper
4 (10-ounce) veal shanks
   (1½ inches thick)
1 tablespoon olive oil
1 cup chopped carrot
1 cup chopped celery
1 cup chopped onion
1 large garlic clove, minced
½ cup dry white wine
1 (14.5-ounce) can diced
   tomatoes, drained
1 tablespoon chopped fresh
   rosemary
½ teaspoon salt
1 bay leaf
Rosemary sprigs (optional)

1. Combine flour and pepper in a pie plate or shallow dish. Dredge veal in flour mixture.
2. Heat oil in a large nonstick skillet over medium-high heat. Add veal; cook 2 minutes on each side or until browned. Place veal in a 4-quart electric slow cooker.
3. Add carrot and next 3 ingredients to pan; sauté over medium heat 5 minutes. Add wine, scraping pan to loosen browned bits. Cook 1 minute. Pour vegetable mixture over veal in cooker. Add tomatoes, chopped rosemary, salt, and bay leaf to cooker; stir well. Cover and cook on LOW 8 to 9 hours or until veal is tender. Discard bay leaf. Garnish with rosemary sprigs, if desired. Yield: 4 servings (serving size: 1 veal shank and 1¼ cups sauce).

CALORIES 397 (26% from fat); FAT 11.6g (sat 2.6g, mono 5.3g, poly 1.4g); PROTEIN 56.4g; CARB 13.9g; FIBER 2.9g; CHOL 213mg; IRON 3mg; SODIUM 641mg; CALC 102mg

Osso buco is a traditional northern Italian dish that usually requires hours in the oven as veal shanks are braised in wine, stock, and tomatoes. The slow cooker makes the ideal cooking environment for veal shanks, which can become tough and dry if not cooked properly. Try spooning the savory sauce over mashed potatoes or soft polenta, or serve with crusty bread to soak up the juices.

(pictured on cover)

Italian Pot Roast with Artichokes and Potatoes

Globe artichokes (*carciofi* in Italian) originated wild in Sicily and are a member of the thistle family. Today, they are cultivated throughout Italy. Tender artichoke hearts are available canned (with the tough leaves and inedible fuzzy choke already removed), which makes them a convenient addition to this hearty meal. Adding them to the slow cooker during the last hour of cooking ensures they will maintain their texture and shape.

4 teaspoons dried Italian seasoning
½ teaspoon salt
½ teaspoon black pepper
1 (3-pound) bone-in center-cut pork loin roast, trimmed and cut in half
2 teaspoons olive oil
½ cup chopped onion
3 garlic cloves, minced
¼ cup fat-free, less-sodium chicken broth
9 small red potatoes (about 1 pound), halved
12 kalamata olives
1 tablespoon capers
1 teaspoon dried oregano
2 (14-ounce) cans whole artichoke hearts (5 to 7 count), drained
Oregano sprigs (optional)

1. Combine Italian seasoning, salt, and pepper; rub over surface of roast. Heat olive oil in a large nonstick skillet over medium-high heat. Add roast; cook 8 minutes, browning on all sides. Remove roast from pan; place in a 6-quart electric slow cooker. Add onion and garlic to pan. Place over medium heat, and sauté 5 minutes. Add broth, scraping pan to loosen browned bits. Pour mixture over roast in cooker.
2. Arrange potatoes and olives around roast; sprinkle with capers and dried oregano. Cover and cook on LOW 9 hours. Add artichoke hearts; cook an additional 1 hour.
3. Place roast on a large platter. Arrange vegetables, olives, and capers around roast. Garnish with oregano sprigs, if desired. Yield: 6 servings (serving size: 3 ounces pork, 3 potato halves, about 2 artichoke hearts, and 2 olives).

CALORIES 354 (29% from fat); FAT 11.5g (sat 3g, mono 6g, poly 1.2g); PROTEIN 37.3g; CARB 24g; FIBER 4.6g; CHOL 93mg; IRON 2.1mg; SODIUM 1,014mg; CALC 52mg

Briny kalamata olives, capers, artichokes, and oregano give traditional pot roast an Italian makeover. To ensure even cooking, cut the roast in half through the two center bones.

Pork with Dried Fruit and Squash

Dried plums (formerly called prunes until they were renamed in 2000 by the California Dried Plum Board) are a good source of antioxidants, iron, and soluble and insoluble fiber. Together with apricots and butternut squash, dried plums make this dish colorful. They also fill it with texture and pack it with nutrition.

1 (3-pound) lean boneless pork loin roast, trimmed
⅓ cup packed brown sugar
1 tablespoon grated peeled fresh ginger
¾ teaspoon salt
½ teaspoon ground cinnamon
¼ teaspoon black pepper
½ cup dried apricots
½ cup bite-sized pitted dried plums
1 (1½-pound) butternut squash, peeled and cubed (about 4 cups)
Rosemary sprigs (optional)

1. Cut pork roast in half crosswise.
2. Combine brown sugar and next 4 ingredients in a small bowl; rub pork evenly with sugar mixture. Place pork in a 4½-quart electric slow cooker. Arrange apricots, dried plums, and squash around pork.
3. Cover and cook on HIGH 1 hour. Reduce heat to LOW, and cook 6 to 7 hours or until pork, fruit, and squash are tender. Cut pork into thin slices, and serve with fruit and squash. Garnish with rosemary sprigs, if desired. Yield: 9 servings (serving size: 3 ounces pork and about ½ cup squash mixture).

CALORIES 320 (22% from fat); FAT 7.7g (sat 2.7g, mono 3.5g, poly 0.9g); PROTEIN 34.5g; CARB 27g; FIBER 2.3g; CHOL 95mg; IRON 2.4mg; SODIUM 301mg; CALC 76mg

After a long day, you'll be welcomed by the aroma of this dish simmering in the slow cooker. A dry rub of brown sugar, ginger, and cinnamon accentuates pork's subtle sweetness. And for a fitting complement, dried fruit plumps up as it cooks with winter squash in the pork's flavorful juices.

Pork Roast with Three-Mushroom Ragoût

To trim excess fat from a roast, hold a sharp knife (chef's knife, paring knife, or boning knife are good choices) parallel to the cutting board, and create a flap by making an incision where the fat connects to the meat. Gently pulling the flap of fat away from the meat, slowly slice back and forth angling the sharp edge of the blade up, rather than down, through the meat. Continue until most of the fat is removed, then discard the fat.

1 (3½-ounce) package shiitake mushrooms
¼ cup all-purpose flour
1 cup canned crushed tomatoes, divided
2 tablespoons chopped fresh or 2 teaspoons dried thyme
2 (8-ounce) packages button mushrooms, cut in half
1 (8-ounce) package cremini mushrooms, cut in half
1 large onion, cut into 8 wedges
½ ounce sun-dried tomatoes, packed without oil, quartered (about 6)
1¾ pounds boned pork loin roast
½ teaspoon salt
¼ teaspoon black pepper
5 cups hot cooked medium egg noodles (about 4 cups uncooked pasta)
Fresh thyme sprigs (optional)

1. Discard shiitake mushroom stems; cut caps into quarters.
2. Lightly spoon flour into a dry measuring cup; level with a knife. Combine flour, ½ cup crushed tomatoes, and thyme in a 5-quart electric slow cooker; stir well with a whisk. Add mushrooms, onion, and sun-dried tomatoes.
3. Trim fat from pork. Sprinkle pork with salt and pepper; place on top of mushroom mixture. Pour remaining ½ cup crushed tomatoes over pork. Cover and cook on HIGH 1 hour. Reduce heat to LOW, and cook 7 hours. Remove pork from cooker; cut into slices. Serve pork and sauce over noodles. Garnish with thyme sprigs, if desired. Yield: 5 servings (serving size: 3 ounces pork, 1 cup sauce, and 1 cup noodles).

CALORIES 460 (22% from fat); FAT 11.2g (sat 3.4g, mono 4.4g, poly 1.8g); PROTEIN 34g; CARB 56g; FIBER 6g; CHOL 117mg; IRON 5.6mg; SODIUM 444mg; CALC 62mg

The term ragoût *comes from the French verb* ragoûter *(which means "to stimulate the appetite") and refers to thick, flavorful stews of meat and vegetables. In this dish, succulent pork in a hearty mushroom-tomato sauce lives up to its name. Three varieties of mushrooms plus fresh thyme offer earthiness, while the sun-dried tomatoes add a sweet punch of flavor. Served over egg noodles or brown rice and paired with a green salad, this dish is special enough for company.*

Apricot and Lamb Tagine

Whole spices like cinnamon sticks do well in a slow cooker because they release their flavor over time. They are removed at the end, leaving behind only their essence. Cinnamon partners particularly well with the spicy-sweet flavors of this dish.

Tagine:
2 cups diced onion (about 1 large)
½ cup orange juice
½ cup less-sodium beef broth
1 tablespoon grated lemon rind
2 tablespoons honey
1 tablespoon fresh lemon juice
2 teaspoons bottled minced garlic
2 teaspoons grated peeled fresh ginger
1½ teaspoons salt
1 teaspoon ground coriander
½ teaspoon ground cumin
¼ teaspoon freshly ground black pepper
2 pounds boneless leg of lamb, trimmed and cut into bite-sized pieces
2 (3-inch) cinnamon sticks
1 (6-ounce) package dried apricots, halved

Remaining Ingredients:
4 cups cooked couscous
¼ cup slivered almonds, toasted
¼ cup chopped fresh parsley

1. To prepare tagine, combine first 15 ingredients in a 4-quart electric slow cooker. Cover and cook on HIGH 1 hour. Reduce heat to LOW, and cook 6 hours. Discard cinnamon sticks.

2. Place ½ cup couscous on each of 8 plates. Top each serving with ½ cup lamb mixture, 1½ teaspoons almonds, and 1½ teaspoons parsley. Yield: 8 servings.

CALORIES 451 (37% from fat); FAT 18.7g (sat 7.1g, mono 8.1g, poly 1.7g); PROTEIN 26.2g; CARB 43.2g; FIBER 3.6g; CHOL 81mg; IRON 3.3mg; SODIUM 515mg; CALC 52mg

In Morocco, the term tagine *refers to any slow-cooked meat or vegetable stew that traditionally has a savory-sweet flavor. It also refers to the earthenware cooking dish in which the stew is cooked and served. A tagine has a platelike bottom with a cone-shaped lid that serves as an ideal vessel for stewing tougher cuts of meat. Here, the slow cooker replaces any specialized equipment and renders a thick lamb stew that fills the air with the exotic aromas of North Africa. Serve this over hot couscous, and sprinkle it with crunchy almonds and chopped fresh parsley for an added bit of texture and fresh flavor.*

poultry

Polynesian Chicken

Browning meat in a skillet before you add it to the slow cooker yields a more attractive color and a richer caramelized flavor that is difficult to achieve in the slow cooker. To determine if the skillet is hot, add a drop of water to the skillet. If the water sizzles and evaporates quickly, the skillet is hot enough to add the chicken pieces. Allow them to cook 3 minutes per side or until the outside is a nice caramel brown.

3 chicken breast halves (about 18 ounces), skinned
6 chicken thighs (about 1¾ pounds), skinned
¼ teaspoon salt
¼ teaspoon black pepper
Cooking spray
1 (8¼-ounce) can pineapple slices in heavy syrup, undrained
1 (8-ounce) can sliced water chestnuts, drained
1 cup fat-free, less-sodium chicken broth
¼ teaspoon ground ginger
1 garlic clove, minced
¼ cup low-sodium soy sauce
¼ cup cornstarch
1 tablespoon white vinegar
½ cup diagonally sliced green onions
6 cups hot cooked rice
6 tablespoons chow mein noodles

1. Sprinkle chicken evenly with salt and pepper. Heat a large nonstick skillet over medium-high heat; coat pan with cooking spray. Add half of chicken pieces; cook 3 minutes on each side or until browned. Repeat procedure with remaining chicken pieces. Place chicken in a 5-quart electric slow cooker.

2. Drain pineapple, reserving syrup. Quarter pineapple slices; arrange pineapple and water chestnuts over chicken. Combine reserved pineapple syrup, chicken broth, ginger, and garlic; pour over chicken.

3. Cover and cook on LOW 8 to 9 hours or until chicken is tender. Remove chicken from cooker with a slotted spoon; keep warm. Reserve cooking liquid in cooker. Increase heat to HIGH.

4. Combine soy sauce, cornstarch, and vinegar in a small bowl, stirring with a whisk until well blended. Stir cornstarch mixture and green onions into cooking liquid in cooker. Cook, uncovered, 10 minutes or until slightly thick, stirring frequently. Serve chicken and sauce over rice on individual plates; top with chow mein noodles. Yield: 6 servings (serving size: 1 chicken breast half or 2 thighs, 1 cup rice, ½ cup sauce, and 1 tablespoon chow mein noodles).

CALORIES 526 (15% from fat); FAT 8.5g (sat 2.2g, mono 3g, poly 2.2g); PROTEIN 34.4g; CARB 74.2g; FIBER 2.6g; CHOL 88mg; IRON 4.4mg; SODIUM 705mg; CALC 34mg

Sweet pineapple, crispy water chestnuts, and crunchy chow mein noodles join to create a lively combination of textures in this island-inspired dish.

Chicken Barbecue

1½ cups sliced onion
½ lemon, sliced and seeded
6 chicken breast halves (about
2¼ pounds), skinned
1 (18-ounce) bottle barbecue
sauce
½ cup cola
½ cup all-purpose flour
½ cup water
Freshly ground black pepper
(optional)

1. Place onion and lemon in a 4-quart electric slow cooker, and top with chicken. Combine barbecue sauce and cola; pour over chicken. Cover and cook on HIGH 1 hour. Reduce heat to LOW, and cook 4 hours or until chicken is tender. Remove chicken and lemon slices from cooker with a slotted spoon, reserving cooking liquid in cooker. Set chicken aside; keep warm. Discard lemon slices. Increase heat to HIGH.

2. Lightly spoon flour into a dry measuring cup; level with a knife. Place flour in a small bowl; gradually add water, stirring with a whisk until well blended. Stir flour mixture into cooking liquid in cooker. Cook, uncovered, 10 minutes or until thick, stirring occasionally. Serve sauce over chicken. Sprinkle with pepper, if desired. Yield: 6 servings (serving size: 1 chicken breast half and ⅔ cup sauce).

CALORIES 244 (11% from fat); FAT 3g (sat 0.6g, mono 1g, poly 0.9g); PROTEIN 28.4g; CARB 24.3g; FIBER 1.7g; CHOL 64mg; IRON 2.1mg; SODIUM 767mg; CALC 36mg

Kitchen shears are a handy tool for removing the skin from poultry quickly and easily. Removing the skin not only reduces the fat grams by about half, but it also gives the dish a more attractive appearance in the end. When working with raw chicken, always rinse the chicken before cooking; then wash your hands, kitchen shears, and cutting board with hot soapy water immediately after use to prevent cross-contamination with other foods.

This weeknight favorite takes its cue from the classic cola-can chicken, where a whole chicken is smoked over an open can of cola to yield flavorful, succulent meat. In the slow-cooker version, we use chicken breasts and add the cola directly to the sauce—the result is just as yummy. Make sure to use regular cola for this recipe. Diet cola won't cook down to the same syrupy consistency. Corn on the cob and a green salad complete the meal.

Saucy Italian-Style Chicken Thighs

12 chicken thighs (about 3 pounds), skinned
1 (14.5-ounce) can Italian-style diced tomatoes, undrained
1 (6-ounce) can tomato paste
½ cup chopped onion
1 tablespoon bottled minced garlic
1 teaspoon dried Italian seasoning
¼ teaspoon salt
¼ teaspoon black pepper

1. Place chicken in a 4-quart electric slow cooker. Combine tomatoes and next 6 ingredients; stir well. Pour sauce over chicken. Cover and cook on HIGH 1 hour. Reduce heat to LOW, and cook 4 to 5 hours or until chicken is tender. Yield: 6 servings (serving size: 2 thighs and about ¾ cup sauce).

CALORIES 202 (24% from fat); FAT 5.4g (sat 1.4g, mono 1.6g, poly 1.4g); PROTEIN 27.8g; CARB 9.6g; FIBER 2.1g; CHOL 109mg; IRON 2.3mg; SODIUM 526mg; CALC 35mg

You don't always have to start from scratch to achieve homemade flavor. Combining Italian-style diced tomatoes with tomato paste yields a simple sauce that, after simmering for hours, develops an intensely rich flavor that is anything but commercial.

Look in your pantry and you'll probably find most of the ingredients needed for this simple and delicious dish. Chicken thighs bring rich flavor and also make for an inexpensive meal. Serve with a slice of crusty bread or over brown rice, spinach fettuccine, or mashed potatoes to soak up the sauce (see pages 140 and 141 for tips on preparing these accompaniments).

Chicken with Figs and Lemon

Calimyrna figs (the California version of Turkish Smyrna figs) are tender and golden-skinned, with tiny seeds and a nutlike flavor. Like other figs, Calimyrnas are extremely perishable, so you're most likely to find them dried, as they're called for in this recipe. For the slow cooker, dried figs are ideal. They plump up, become tender, and maintain their shape after simmering for hours in the sauce.

8 chicken thighs (about 2¼ pounds), skinned
1 cup fat-free, less-sodium chicken broth
½ teaspoon grated lemon rind
3 tablespoons fresh lemon juice
1 (1.25-ounce) package creamy garlic Alfredo pasta sauce mix (such as McCormick)
3 tablespoons Dijon mustard
4 garlic cloves, minced, or 4 teaspoons bottled minced garlic
1 cup sliced onion
1 cup dried Calimyrna figs, halved
Fresh thyme sprigs (optional)

1. Brown chicken thighs in a skillet over medium-high heat 5 to 6 minutes, turning once.
2. Combine broth and next 5 ingredients in a 4½-quart electric slow cooker; stir mixture until well blended. Add onion, fig halves, and chicken, pushing chicken pieces down into broth mixture.
3. Cover and cook on LOW 6 to 8 hours or until chicken and figs are tender. Serve with sauce. Garnish with thyme, if desired. Yield: 4 servings (serving size: 2 thighs and ¾ cup sauce).

CALORIES 431 (33% from fat); FAT 15.9g (sat 5.3g, mono 4.8g, poly 3g); PROTEIN 34.1g; CARB 38.9g; FIBER 5.4g; CHOL 119mg; IRON 3.3mg; SODIUM 819mg; CALC 107mg

Lemon, dried figs, Dijon mustard, and garlic infuse saucy chicken thighs in this Mediterranean-inspired dish. Squeeze a fresh lemon and mince the garlic yourself to add the freshest flavors, and then save time with canned broth and a package of Alfredo sauce mix. This balance of quality produce enhanced with convenience products takes quick and easy cooking to a new level. Serve over a bed of couscous and add another hint of freshness with a sprig of fresh thyme (see page 140 for information on preparing couscous).

Lemon-Pepper Turkey Breast

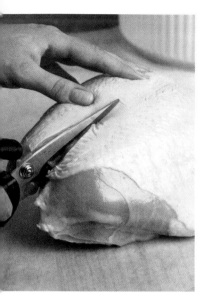

1 (5-pound) bone-in turkey
  breast, skinned and cut in
  half
2 teaspoons lemon pepper
2 tablespoons all-purpose
  flour
3 tablespoons water

1. Sprinkle turkey evenly with lemon pepper. Place turkey breast halves, meaty sides down, in a 5-quart electric slow cooker. Cover and cook on HIGH 1 hour. Reduce heat to LOW; cook 5 hours or until turkey is tender. Remove turkey to a platter, reserving cooking liquid in cooker. Set turkey aside; keep warm.

2. Combine flour and water in a medium saucepan, stirring with a whisk until well blended. Gradually add reserved cooking liquid, stirring constantly. Bring to a boil over medium-high heat, stirring constantly. Reduce heat, and simmer 4 minutes or until thick, stirring occasionally. Serve turkey with gravy. Yield: 9 servings (serving size: 6 ounces turkey and 2 tablespoons gravy).

CALORIES 227 (5% from fat); FAT 1.3g (sat 0.4g, mono 0.2g, poly 0.4g); PROTEIN 49.2g; CARB 1.3g; FIBER 0.1g; CHOL 123mg; IRON 2.4mg; SODIUM 124mg; CALC 20mg

When using a slow cooker, you should cut any piece of meat or poultry that's over 3 pounds in half to ensure thorough cooking. Use kitchen shears to halve the turkey breast, or ask your butcher to halve it at the store. Or buy two 2½-pound turkey breast halves instead. Be sure to remove the skin before cooking.

With only four ingredients, this juicy turkey-and-gravy feast is hard to beat. Prepare and serve it as the centerpiece to a grand meal, and save the oven for all of those side dishes. Or you can go casual and serve sliced leftover turkey and gravy on toasted rolls for a sublime experience. Either way, you'll never look at your slow cooker the same way.

Turkey Thighs with Olives and Dried Cherries

Crushed red pepper, a familiar favorite in pizza parlors, is made from the same kind of dried chili pepper that is ground to make cayenne pepper. It has a smoky heat that hits in the mouth and throat with a subtle floral hint. It balances well with the sweet flavors of port, cherries, and orange juice in this recipe. Check the freshness of crushed red pepper by rubbing the flakes in your hand. If no aroma is detected, they may have lost some of their heat.

1 cup thinly sliced leek (about 1 large)
1 cup ruby port or other sweet red wine
¾ cup dried cherries
¾ cup pitted kalamata olives
⅓ cup fresh orange juice (about 1 orange)
1 teaspoon paprika
1 teaspoon crushed red pepper
4 thyme sprigs
1 (3-inch) cinnamon stick
1½ teaspoons salt, divided
3½ pounds turkey thighs, skinned
1 tablespoon ground cumin

1. Combine first 9 ingredients in a 6-quart oval electric slow cooker. Stir in ½ teaspoon salt.

2. Rinse turkey with cold water; pat dry. Sprinkle with remaining 1 teaspoon salt and cumin. Place in cooker. Cover and cook on HIGH 1 hour. Reduce heat to LOW, and cook 4 hours. Discard cinnamon stick. Yield: 6 servings (serving size: 5 ounces turkey and about ½ cup leek mixture).

CALORIES 419 (34% from fat); FAT 16.1g (sat 4.7g, mono 5.5g, poly 4.1g); PROTEIN 32.5g; CARB 23.1g; FIBER 2.9g; CHOL 101mg; IRON 4.1mg; SODIUM 1,453mg; CALC 61mg

The sophisticated combination of earthy, spicy, and sweet flavors in this entrée will wow your dinner guests. Turkey thighs are easy to find, but you also can use skinless chicken thighs, if you prefer. Serve with mashed potatoes or couscous for a rustic yet impressive meal (recipes on pages 140 and 141).

Tiny French Beans with Smoked Sausage

Flageolets, or tiny French kidney beans, are tender with a delicate flavor. Their colors range from pale green to off-white. They are rarely available fresh in the U.S., but the dried form can be found at specialty food stores. Substitute any dried white bean for the flageolets in the recipe and enjoy the rare pleasure of beans that have cooked all day. Although canned beans offer convenience when you're busy, take advantage of the slow cooker's hands-off ability to cook dried beans without the fuss of presoaking.

2 pounds smoked turkey sausage, cut into 1½-inch pieces
1 tablespoon canola oil
⅓ cup minced shallots
3 garlic cloves, minced
2 cups dried flageolets or other dried white beans (about 1 pound)
2 cups water
¼ cup minced fresh or 1 tablespoon dried thyme
1 teaspoon celery seeds
¼ teaspoon freshly ground black pepper
2 (14-ounce) cans fat-free, less-sodium chicken broth
Fresh thyme sprigs (optional)

1. Heat a large nonstick skillet over medium heat. Add sausage; sauté 5 minutes or until browned. Remove from pan; place in a 5-quart electric slow cooker. Heat oil in pan over medium heat. Add shallots and garlic; sauté 1 minute.
2. Sort and wash beans. Add beans, shallot mixture, water, and next 4 ingredients to cooker. Cover and cook on HIGH 8 hours or until beans are tender. Garnish with thyme sprigs, if desired. Yield: 8 servings (serving size: 1¼ cups).

CALORIES 366 (33% from fat); FAT 13.6g (sat 3.2g, mono 5.1g, poly 3.6g); PROTEIN 27.3g; CARB 34.9g; FIBER 0.3g; CHOL 75mg; IRON 4.4mg; SODIUM 1,362mg; CALC 92mg

Smoked sausage and white beans simmer all day in a broth infused with shallots, garlic, and thyme. This is a hearty meal you'll be happy to come home to. Uncork a bottle of robust red wine and curl up with a bowlful of instant comfort.

Red Beans and Rice

The bay leaf, a bold, fragrant herb that comes from the evergreen bay laurel tree, imparts a wonderful lemon-nutmeg flavor when simmered in soups or when cooked with meat or vegetables. Fresh bay leaves, though more flavorful and flexible, can be hard to find, so if you can't locate them, the dried variety will work just fine. Be sure to remove bay leaves before you serve your dish—the leaves are bitter and difficult to chew.

3 cups water
1 cup dried red kidney beans
1 cup chopped onion
1 cup chopped green bell pepper
¾ cup chopped celery
1 teaspoon dried thyme
1 teaspoon paprika
¾ teaspoon ground red pepper
½ teaspoon black pepper
½ (14-ounce) package turkey, pork, and beef smoked sausage (such as Healthy Choice), thinly sliced
1 bay leaf
5 garlic cloves, minced
½ teaspoon salt
3 cups hot cooked long-grain rice
¼ cup chopped green onions

1. Combine first 12 ingredients in a 2-quart electric slow cooker. Cover and cook on HIGH 5 hours. Discard bay leaf; stir in salt. Serve over rice in individual bowls; sprinkle evenly with green onions. Yield: 4 servings (serving size: 1 cup bean mixture, ¾ cup rice, and 1 tablespoon green onions).

CALORIES 413 (5% from fat); FAT 2.5g (sat 0.7g, mono 0.2g, poly 0.5g); PROTEIN 21.1g; CARB 76.3g; FIBER 10.1g; CHOL 18mg; IRON 6mg; SODIUM 749mg; CALC 102mg

This traditional Louisiana Creole fare is the ultimate in thriftiness and convenience. The long cooking time coaxes the spiciness from the sausage into the beans. Be sure to add the salt to the dish after it has cooked and just before serving. Adding salt to dried beans too early will slow the cooking process and make the beans less tender. Served over rice with a side of slaw, this southern classic is hard to beat.

vegetarian

Pesto Lasagna with Spinach and Mushrooms

No-boil (or "oven ready") lasagna noodles have a porous texture that allows the noodles to absorb liquid from other ingredients as they bake, eliminating the need to boil them. This product is not only convenient, but the noodles will also soak up the extra liquid that accumulates in the slow cooker.

4 cups torn spinach
2 cups sliced cremini mushrooms
½ cup commercial pesto
¾ cup (3 ounces) shredded part-skim mozzarella cheese
¾ cup (3 ounces) shredded provolone cheese
1 (15-ounce) carton fat-free ricotta cheese
1 large egg, lightly beaten
¾ cup (3 ounces) grated fresh Parmesan cheese, divided
1 (26-ounce) jar fat-free tomato-basil pasta sauce
1 (8-ounce) can tomato sauce
Cooking spray
1 (8-ounce) package precooked lasagna noodles

1. Steam spinach, covered, 3 minutes or until spinach wilts. Drain, squeeze dry, and coarsely chop. Combine spinach, mushrooms, and pesto in a medium bowl, and set aside.

2. Combine mozzarella, provolone, ricotta, and egg in a medium bowl, stirring well. Stir in ¼ cup Parmesan cheese, and set aside. Combine pasta sauce and tomato sauce in a medium bowl.

3. Spread 1 cup pasta sauce mixture in bottom of a 6-quart oval electric slow cooker coated with cooking spray. Arrange 3 noodles over pasta sauce mixture, and top with 1 cup cheese mixture and 1 cup spinach mixture. Repeat layers once, ending with remaining 1 cup spinach mixture. Arrange 3 noodles over spinach mixture; top with remaining cheese mixture and 1 cup pasta sauce mixture. Place 3 noodles over sauce mixture; spread remaining sauce mixture over noodles. Sprinkle with remaining ½ cup Parmesan cheese. Cover and cook on LOW 5 hours or until done. Yield: 8 servings.

CALORIES 398 (41% from fat); FAT 18.2g (sat 7.8g, mono 6.6g, poly 2.3g); PROTEIN 22.2g; CARB 38.5g; FIBER 2g; CHOL 56mg; IRON 2.8mg; SODIUM 1,036mg; CALC 407mg

Earthy pesto, spinach, and cremini mushrooms add body and heartiness to meatless lasagna. To make the dish even easier to prepare, use 2 (10-ounce) packages of frozen chopped spinach in place of fresh. Just be sure to drain the defrosted spinach well by squeezing it dry. Feel free to substitute any mushroom you like for the cremini.

Barley, Black Bean, and Corn Burritos

Vegetable broth is an excellent choice to flavor soups, stews, and grains (like the pearl barley in this recipe) when you want to keep a dish vegetarian. Flavored with vegetables and seasonings, it provides much of the flavor of chicken or beef broth without the meat base. Look for certified organic vegetable broth (such as Swanson); this kind has ⅓ less sodium than regular canned vegetable broth, and it has a superior flavor.

1 (15-ounce) can black beans, rinsed and drained
1 (10-ounce) can diced tomatoes and green chiles, undrained
1 cup uncooked pearl barley
2 cups organic vegetable broth (such as Swanson Certified Organic)
¾ cup frozen whole-kernel corn
¼ cup chopped green onions
1 tablespoon fresh lime juice
1 teaspoon ground cumin
1 teaspoon chili powder
½ teaspoon ground red pepper
1 garlic clove, minced
¼ cup chopped fresh cilantro
18 (6½-inch) flour tortillas
1 cup plus 2 tablespoons (4½ ounces) shredded reduced-fat sharp Cheddar cheese
9 cups thinly sliced curly leaf lettuce
2¼ cups salsa
1 cup plus 2 tablespoons fat-free sour cream

1. Place first 11 ingredients in a 3- to 4-quart electric slow cooker; stir well. Cover and cook on LOW 4 to 5 hours or until barley is tender. Stir in cilantro.
2. Heat tortillas according to package directions. Spoon ⅓ cup barley mixture down center of each tortilla; sprinkle each with 1 tablespoon cheese. Roll up. Place 1 cup lettuce on each of 9 plates; top each with 2 burritos. Spoon ¼ cup salsa and 2 tablespoons sour cream over each serving. Yield: 9 servings.

CALORIES 402 (19% from fat); FAT 8.5g (sat 3.3g, mono 0.1g, poly 0.3g); PROTEIN 15.6g; CARB 70.1g; FIBER 10.2g; CHOL 14mg; IRON 2.1mg; SODIUM 1,181mg; CALC 263mg

There's no need to go out to the local cantina when this wholesome Mexican-style meal is waiting for you at home. Protein-packed black beans and fiber-filled barley come together in this healthy substitute for meat-based burritos. Spicy tomatoes with green chiles, lime juice, cumin, and chili powder add south-of-the-border flavor and intensity.

Barley-Stuffed Cabbage Rolls with Pine Nuts and Currants

To core a cabbage head, place it, stem side up, on a cutting board. Using a chef's knife, cut a cone-shaped hole around the core about 4 inches wide and 3 inches deep; remove and discard the core. After steaming the cabbage head, remove the leaves, and trim away the raised portion of the thick center vein from each leaf. This makes the leaves more pliable and easier to roll up. Be careful to leave the rest of the vein intact.

1 large head green cabbage, cored
1 tablespoon olive oil
1½ cups finely chopped onion
3 cups cooked pearl barley
¾ cup (3 ounces) crumbled feta cheese
½ cup dried currants
2 tablespoons pine nuts, toasted
2 tablespoons chopped fresh parsley
½ teaspoon salt, divided
¼ teaspoon black pepper, divided
½ cup apple juice
1 tablespoon cider vinegar
1 (14.5-ounce) can crushed tomatoes, undrained

1. Steam cabbage head, covered, 8 minutes; cool slightly. Remove 16 leaves from cabbage head; reserve remaining leaves for another use. Cut off raised portion of center vein of each cabbage leaf (do not cut out vein); set trimmed cabbage leaves aside.
2. Heat oil in a large nonstick skillet over medium heat. Add onion; cover and cook 6 minutes or until tender. Remove from heat; stir in barley and next 4 ingredients. Stir in ¼ teaspoon salt and ⅛ teaspoon pepper.
3. Place cabbage leaves on a flat surface; spoon about ⅓ cup barley mixture into center of each cabbage leaf. Fold in edges of leaves over barley mixture; roll up. Arrange cabbage rolls in bottom of a 5-quart electric slow cooker.
4. Combine remaining ¼ teaspoon salt, remaining ⅛ teaspoon pepper, apple juice, vinegar, and tomatoes; pour evenly over cabbage rolls. Cover and cook on HIGH 2 hours or until thoroughly heated. Yield: 4 servings (serving size: 4 cabbage rolls and 2 tablespoons sauce).

CALORIES 402 (25% from fat); FAT 11.3g (sat 4.2g, mono 4.4g, poly 1.9g); PROTEIN 11.3g; CARB 70.1g; FIBER 11.3g; CHOL 19mg; IRON 5mg; SODIUM 693mg; CALC 234mg

The combination of barley, currants, and pine nuts brings a variety of flavors and textures to this elegant dish. Assemble the rolls the night before, and you'll have a great head start on the next day's dinner.

Hoppin' John

Rice can be particularly tricky to cook in a slow cooker. For the best results, always use converted (parboiled) rice. Converted rice is simply rice that has undergone a steaming process before being dried and hulled. This process makes for a fluffier texture and transfers some of the nutrients from the hull to the grain. Converted rice is slightly beige and takes a little longer to cook than regular white rice.

2 (16-ounce) packages frozen black-eyed peas
2 cups hot water
¾ cup sliced green onions
¾ cup chopped red bell pepper
2 tablespoons minced seeded jalapeño pepper
2 teaspoons hot sauce
½ teaspoon salt
¼ teaspoon black pepper
1 vegetable-flavored bouillon cube
1 (14.5-ounce) can Cajun-style stewed tomatoes with pepper, garlic, and Cajun spices, undrained
⅔ cup uncooked converted rice
½ cup sliced green onions

1. Combine first 9 ingredients in a 4-quart electric slow cooker, and stir well. Cover and cook on HIGH 4 hours. Stir in tomatoes and rice, and cover and cook 1 hour or until peas and rice are tender and most of liquid is absorbed. Stir in ½ cup green onions. Yield: 6 servings (serving size: 1⅔ cups).

CALORIES 326 (4% from fat); FAT 1.6g (sat 0.5g, mono 0.1g, poly 0.5g); PROTEIN 16.1g; CARB 63g; FIBER 9.9g; CHOL 0mg; IRON 4.5mg; SODIUM 754mg; CALC 76mg

A South Carolina Low-Country specialty, hoppin' John is said to bring good luck and prosperity all year when eaten on New Year's Day. This budget-friendly dish traditionally includes ham hocks, but you'll find the meatless combination of rice, tomatoes, and black-eyed peas filling, nutritious, and full of flavor.

Vegetable and Chickpea Curry

1 tablespoon olive oil
1½ cups chopped onion
1 cup (¼-inch-thick) slices carrot
1 tablespoon curry powder
1 teaspoon brown sugar
1 teaspoon grated peeled fresh ginger
2 garlic cloves, minced
1 serrano chile, seeded and minced
3 cups cooked chickpeas (garbanzo beans)
1½ cups cubed peeled baking potato
1 cup coarsely chopped green bell pepper
1 cup (1-inch) cut green beans
½ teaspoon salt
¼ teaspoon black pepper
⅛ teaspoon ground red pepper
1 (14.5-ounce) can diced tomatoes, undrained
1 (14-ounce) can vegetable broth
3 cups fresh baby spinach
1 cup light coconut milk
6 lemon wedges

1. Heat oil in a large nonstick skillet over medium heat. Add onion and carrot; cover and cook 5 minutes or until tender. Add curry powder and next 4 ingredients; cook 1 minute, stirring constantly.

2. Place onion mixture in a 5-quart electric slow cooker. Stir in chickpeas and next 8 ingredients. Cover and cook on HIGH 6 hours or until vegetables are tender. Add spinach and coconut milk; stir until spinach wilts. Serve with lemon wedges. Yield: 6 servings (serving size: 1⅓ cups vegetable mixture and 1 lemon wedge).

CALORIES 276 (23% from fat); FAT 7.2g (sat 1.9g, mono 2.3g, poly 1.3g); PROTEIN 10.9g; CARB 44.7g; FIBER 10.6g; CHOL 0mg; IRON 4.3mg; SODIUM 623mg; CALC 107mg

Fresh, delicate baby spinach won't hold up to long hours of slow cooking. Simply stir the mild greens into the curry at the last minute; the leaves will quickly wilt. Baby spinach is convenient because its stems are tender and do not need to be removed. This last-minute addition gives this curry a boost of nutrients, including beta-carotene, potassium, and vitamin A.

Aromatic Indian spices mingle with chickpeas, green beans, and potatoes. Coconut milk is stirred into the cooked curry for a creamy finish. Feel free to substitute or add whatever vegetables are in season. Try serving it over quick-cooking couscous, and top with a simple Indian raita made from yogurt and chopped cucumber. The cooling sauce will balance the spiciness of the curry. For tips on cooking your own beans, see page 141, or substitute two 15½-ounce cans of chickpeas, rinsed and drained.

Thyme-Scented White Bean Cassoulet

Meatless sausage stands in here for the traditional pork sausage. Meatless sausage primarily contains soy protein, which is low in saturated fat. It has no cholesterol and is a good source of fiber, iron, and zinc. This ingredient does not need to cook for long hours. Adding the thawed sausage to the hot bean mixture at the end is enough. But you can first sauté it in a nonstick skillet over medium-high heat for 2 to 3 minutes, if desired, for a more appealing browned appearance.

1 tablespoon olive oil
1½ cups chopped onion
1½ cups (½-inch-thick) slices diagonally cut carrot
1 cup (½-inch-thick) slices diagonally cut parsnip
2 garlic cloves, minced
3 cups cooked Great Northern beans
¾ cup vegetable broth
½ teaspoon dried thyme
¼ teaspoon salt
¼ teaspoon black pepper
1 (28-ounce) can diced tomatoes, undrained
1 bay leaf
¼ cup dry breadcrumbs
¼ cup (1 ounce) grated fresh Parmesan cheese
2 tablespoons butter, melted
2 links frozen meatless Italian sausage (such as Boca), thawed and chopped
2 tablespoons chopped fresh parsley

1. Heat olive oil in a large nonstick skillet over medium heat. Add onion, carrot, parsnip, and garlic; cover and cook 5 minutes.
2. Place parsnip mixture in a 5-quart electric slow cooker. Add beans and next 6 ingredients. Cover and cook on LOW 8 hours or until vegetables are tender. Discard bay leaf.
3. Combine breadcrumbs, cheese, and butter in a small bowl; toss with a fork until moist. Stir breadcrumb mixture and sausage into bean mixture; sprinkle with parsley. Yield: 6 servings (serving size: 1⅓ cups).

CALORIES 314 (29% from fat); FAT 10.2g (sat 3.7g, mono 3.7g, poly 1.7g); PROTEIN 16.4g; CARB 41.9g; FIBER 11.6g; CHOL 13mg; IRON 3.6mg; SODIUM 777mg; CALC 177mg

Butter-tossed breadcrumbs that are stirred in just before serving give this dish a robust stewlike consistency. This is a hearty meal for a cold winter's day. See page 141 for guidelines on cooking beans, or you can substitute two 16-ounce cans of Great Northern beans, rinsed and drained.

Pinto Bean Chili with Corn and Winter Squash

Queso fresco, a Mexican white cheese made from cow's milk, has a fine-grained, crumbly texture and a mild, slightly salty flavor. When heated, it becomes creamy but does not melt—a characteristic of Mexican fresh cheeses. This cheese's mild flavor complements the spicy chili. Queso fresco, also found labeled *queso blanco,* is available in many large supermarkets. If you can't find it, substitute crumbled feta or farmer cheese.

1 tablespoon olive oil
1½ cups chopped onion
1½ cups chopped red bell pepper
1 garlic clove, minced
2 tablespoons chili powder
½ teaspoon ground cumin
4 cups (½-inch) cubed peeled butternut squash (about 1 pound)
2 (16-ounce) cans pinto beans, rinsed and drained
1½ cups water
1 cup frozen whole-kernel corn
1 teaspoon salt
1 (28-ounce) can crushed tomatoes, undrained
1 (4.5-ounce) can chopped green chiles, undrained
¾ cup (3 ounces) crumbled queso fresco
12 lime wedges

1. Heat oil in a large nonstick skillet over medium heat. Add onion, bell pepper, and garlic; cover and cook 5 minutes or until tender. Add chili powder and cumin; cook 1 minute, stirring constantly.
2. Place onion mixture in a 5-quart electric slow cooker. Add squash and next 6 ingredients. Cover and cook on LOW 8 hours or until chili is thick. Ladle chili into individual bowls. Sprinkle with cheese, and serve with lime wedges. Yield: 6 servings (serving size: 1¾ cups chili, 2 tablespoons cheese, and 2 lime wedges).

CALORIES 319 (17% from fat); FAT 6.1g (sat 2g, mono 2.5g, poly 1.3g); PROTEIN 14.3g; CARB 56g; FIBER 12.7g; CHOL 10mg; IRON 4.4mg; SODIUM 862mg; CALC 255mg

The spiciness of this light yet satisfying chili is complemented by the subtle sweetness of corn and winter squash. For a heartier chili, add 1 cup of thawed frozen meatless crumbles. For a vegan version, use shredded soy Cheddar or soy mozzarella cheese.

African Sweet Potato Stew with Red Beans

Although peanut butter is high in fat, a little of this high-flavor favorite goes a long way. The fat can act as a binding agent in sauces and stews and can stand in for cream to thicken sauces and gravies. In this stew, peanut butter's nutty flavor complements a variety of spicy and smoky ingredients, such as cumin, ginger, and green chiles.

2 teaspoons olive oil
1½ cups chopped onion
1 garlic clove, minced
4 cups (½-inch) cubed peeled sweet potato (about 1½ pounds)
1½ cups cooked small red beans
1½ cups vegetable broth
1 cup chopped red bell pepper
½ cup water
1 teaspoon grated peeled fresh ginger
½ teaspoon salt
½ teaspoon ground cumin
¼ teaspoon black pepper
1 (14.5-ounce) can diced tomatoes, drained
1 (4.5-ounce) can chopped green chiles, drained
3 tablespoons creamy peanut butter
3 tablespoons chopped dry-roasted peanuts
6 lime wedges

1. Heat oil in a nonstick skillet over medium heat. Add onion and garlic; cover and cook 5 minutes or until tender.
2. Place onion mixture in a 5-quart electric slow cooker. Add sweet potato and next 10 ingredients. Cover and cook on LOW 8 hours or until vegetables are tender.
3. Spoon 1 cup cooking liquid into a small bowl. Add peanut butter; stir well with a whisk. Stir peanut butter mixture into stew. Ladle stew into individual bowls. Top with peanuts; serve with lime wedges. Yield: 6 servings (serving size: 1⅓ cups stew, 1½ teaspoons peanuts, and 1 lime wedge).

CALORIES 308 (26% from fat); FAT 8.8g (sat 1.5g, mono 4.2g, poly 2.3g); PROTEIN 11.1g; CARB 49.9g; FIBER 10.2g; CHOL 0mg; IRON 2.7mg; SODIUM 574mg; CALC 64mg

Vivid colors and fragrant spices are the hallmarks of this thick stew, which is garnished with crunchy peanuts. A squeeze of lime juice brightens the rich, earthy flavors. For tips on how to cook your own beans, see page 141, or substitute one 16-ounce can of red beans, rinsed and drained.

soups & stews

Spicy Black and Red Bean Soup

Shoepeg corn is a sweet white corn named for the wooden pegs used to attach soles to shoes in the nineteenth century. The white kernels are small and narrow, and they have a sweet, milky flavor. Also called Country Gentleman, this variety of corn can be difficult to find fresh, but it's widely available canned or frozen. Shoepeg corn makes a delicious addition to salads, salsas, side dishes, and soups like this one.

1½ cups chopped onion
1¼ cups sliced carrot
2 garlic cloves, minced
3 cups fat-free, less-sodium chicken broth
2 teaspoons sugar
1 (16-ounce) package frozen shoepeg white corn
1 (16-ounce) can red beans or kidney beans, drained
1 (15-ounce) can black beans, drained
1 (14.5-ounce) can Mexican-style stewed tomatoes with jalapeño peppers and spices, undrained
1 (14.5-ounce) can no salt–added diced tomatoes, undrained
1 (4.5-ounce) can chopped green chiles, undrained

1. Combine all ingredients in a 5- or 6-quart electric slow cooker. Cover and cook on LOW 8 hours. Yield: 10 servings (serving size: 1 cup).

CALORIES 142 (6% from fat); FAT 0.9g (sat 0g, mono 0g, poly 0.1g); PROTEIN 6.5g; CARB 28.7g; FIBER 6.5g; CHOL 0mg; IRON 1.2mg; SODIUM 503mg; CALC 57mg

Stir in shredded cooked chicken or browned ground beef to add more protein. Or make this versatile soup vegetarian by substituting vegetable broth for the chicken broth. Leftovers freeze well, but this soup is so tasty that you might not have much left!

Chunky Minestrone

For the best texture, you should cook pasta outside the slow cooker unless the recipe directs otherwise. However, with a few guidelines, soups are good candidates for cooking pasta directly in the cooker. Small pastas like ditalini, tubetti, and the small seashell pasta shown above are good choices for soups. The pasta needs to cook longer than it would on the stovetop because the soup will not come to a rolling boil in your slow cooker. It will be overcooked, however, if you put it in at the beginning. Adding the pasta just before the last 30 minutes allows it the right amount of time to cook.

3 (14-ounce) cans fat-free, less-sodium chicken broth
2 (14.5-ounce) cans no salt–added diced tomatoes with roasted garlic, undrained
1 (15.5-ounce) can cannellini beans or other white beans, rinsed and drained
1 (10-ounce) package frozen chopped spinach, thawed
1 cup water
1½ cups frozen chopped onion, thawed
1 medium carrot, chopped
1 medium zucchini, quartered and sliced
2 teaspoons olive oil
1 teaspoon dried Italian seasoning
¼ teaspoon black pepper
½ cup uncooked small seashell pasta
⅔ cup (2.5 ounces) freshly grated Parmesan cheese

1. Combine first 11 ingredients in a 4-quart electric slow cooker. Cover and cook on LOW 5½ hours.
2. Add pasta; cover and cook on LOW 30 minutes. Ladle soup into individual bowls. Sprinkle with cheese. Yield: 5 servings (serving size: 2⅓ cups soup and 2 tablespoons cheese).

CALORIES 284 (27% from fat); FAT 8.4g (sat 3.6g, mono 1.4g, poly 0.6g); PROTEIN 16.4g; CARB 37.4g; FIBER 6.7g; CHOL 16mg; IRON 3.6mg; SODIUM 602mg; CALC 381mg

In Italian, minestrone means "big soup." This filling combination of beans, fresh and frozen vegetables, and pasta lives up to the name. Vegetables lose their crunch when they're frozen, so using frozen chopped onion ensures that the onion won't still be crunchy after cooking. If you'd rather use fresh, microwave chopped fresh onion at HIGH for a minute or two to precook it a little.

Homestyle Potato Soup

Cheddar cheese's sharpness contrasts well with mild potato soup, making it an ideal topping. The sharper the cheese, the better, since you can use less of it for the same amount of flavor. When you're shredding Cheddar, use the largest holes of a box grater to get long shreds.

4 cups cubed peeled baking potato
1 cup chopped onion
1 cup thinly sliced celery
¾ cup thinly sliced carrot
3 tablespoons butter, cut into small pieces
1¼ teaspoons salt
½ teaspoon freshly ground black pepper
1 (14-ounce) can vegetable broth
3 garlic cloves, minced
¼ cup all-purpose flour
1½ cups 2% reduced-fat milk
7 tablespoons shredded reduced-fat sharp Cheddar cheese
Freshly ground black pepper (optional)

1. Place first 9 ingredients in a 4½-quart electric slow cooker; stir well. Cover and cook on LOW 6 to 7 hours or until vegetables are tender. Increase heat to HIGH.

2. Lightly spoon flour into a dry measuring cup; level with a knife. Place flour in a bowl; gradually add milk, stirring with a whisk until well blended. Stir into soup. Cook, uncovered, 25 minutes or until thick, stirring frequently. Ladle soup into individual bowls, and sprinkle with cheese and additional pepper, if desired. Yield: 7 servings (serving size: 1 cup soup and 1 tablespoon cheese).

CALORIES 194 (35% from fat); FAT 7.6g (sat 4.8g, mono 1.6g, poly 0.3g); PROTEIN 5.9g; CARB 26.8g; FIBER 2.2g; CHOL 22mg; IRON 0.7mg; SODIUM 801mg; CALC 151mg

Nothing soothes the soul on a cold day like a warm bowl of potato soup. With carrots, celery, and garlic, this chunky version is big on flavor. We've lowered the fat in this recipe while maintaining taste and texture by using reduced-fat (but not fat-free) milk and cheese.

Caribbean Seafood Pot

When the flavor of olive oil isn't needed for a recipe, canola oil (instead of regular vegetable oil) is the best choice in terms of health benefits. Canola oil contains mostly unsaturated fats and, next to olive oil, it has the most monounsaturated fat. It's also a valuable source of omega-3 fatty acids, which are essential to a heart-healthy diet.

2 teaspoons canola oil
2 cups diced peeled red potato
1 cup chopped onion
¾ cup diced red bell pepper
⅔ cup chopped celery
4 garlic cloves, minced
2 (14.5-ounce) cans diced tomatoes with garlic and onion, undrained
2 (8-ounce) bottles clam juice
3 tablespoons pickled jalapeño pepper slices, minced
1 teaspoon dried thyme
¼ teaspoon ground allspice
¾ pound grouper or other firm white fish fillet, cut into 1-inch cubes
¾ pound large shrimp, peeled

1. Heat oil in a large nonstick skillet over medium-high heat. Add potato and next 3 ingredients; sauté 5 minutes. Add garlic, and sauté 30 seconds. Cover, reduce heat to medium, and cook 5 minutes or until potato is tender. Place potato mixture in a 4½-quart electric slow cooker. Add tomatoes and next 4 ingredients; stir well. Cover and cook on LOW 7 hours.

2. Add grouper and shrimp; cover and cook 10 minutes or until shrimp are done and fish flakes easily when tested with a fork. Yield: 6 servings (serving size: 1¾ cups).

CALORIES 226 (18% from fat); FAT 4.4g (sat 0.5g, mono 1.2g, poly 1.1g); PROTEIN 26.8g; CARB 21g; FIBER 3.2g; CHOL 109mg; IRON 4.8mg; SODIUM 1,025mg; CALC 99mg

Grouper is a mild fish that takes on the flavor of the seasonings in which it cooks, so don't worry about this filling stew being too fishy. Don't add the shrimp and fish to the cooker until the last 10 minutes; they don't need to cook long.

Vegetable-Beef Soup

If you prefer even more zip in this soup, reach for a spicy herb blend instead of more salt. A salt-free herb blend contains onion, garlic, dried tomato, and a wide variety of spices, so it adds a lot of flavor without adding any sodium. No matter how much you use, the nutritional analysis will stay the same.

¼ cup all-purpose flour
1½ pounds lean top round steak, cut into 1-inch cubes
Cooking spray
2 teaspoons spicy herb blend (such as Mrs. Dash Extra Spicy Seasoning Blend)
2 (16-ounce) packages frozen gumbo vegetable mix
1 (10-ounce) package frozen chopped onion
2 (14.5-ounce) cans diced tomatoes with garlic, undrained
2 (14-ounce) cans fat-free, less-sodium beef broth
1 tablespoon bottled minced garlic
1 tablespoon low-sodium Worcestershire sauce
½ teaspoon salt
½ teaspoon black pepper

1. Place flour in a large zip-top plastic bag; add steak cubes. Seal and shake to coat. Remove steak from bag, and set aside.

2. Place a large nonstick skillet over medium-high heat until hot; coat pan with cooking spray. Add steak, and cook until browned on all sides.

3. Place steak and remaining ingredients in a 5-quart electric slow cooker; stir well. Cover and cook on HIGH 1 hour; reduce heat to LOW, and cook 6 hours or until steak is done and vegetables are tender. Yield: 8 servings (serving size: about 1¾ cups).

CALORIES 256 (20% from fat); FAT 5.6g (sat 2g, mono 2.2g, poly 0.4g); PROTEIN 26g; CARB 26g; FIBER 6.2g; CHOL 49mg; IRON 3.4mg; SODIUM 542mg; CALC 66mg

Convenience products eliminate most of the prep work for this easy recipe. For a classic comfort-food combo, serve this soup with half of a grilled cheese sandwich made with whole wheat bread and reduced-fat cheese.

Hearty Vegetable–Smoked Sausage Soup

Contrary to popular belief, peeling potatoes does not remove valuable nutrients. These nutrients—including vitamins B6 and C, niacin, potassium, thiamin, and zinc—are located about ½ inch below a potato's skin. Peeling potatoes does allow more starch, a thickening agent, to be released into the soup's broth. Baking potatoes, often called Idaho potatoes, are ideal for this soup because they are full of starch. Red-skinned potatoes are too waxy for this recipe and won't produce the same thick broth.

1 (14-ounce) package low-fat smoked sausage, cut into ¼-inch-thick slices
2¾ cups (½-inch) cubed peeled baking potato
½ (10-ounce) package angel hair slaw (about 4 cups)
2 cups chopped onion
1 cup sliced carrot
1⅓ cups diced celery
1 cup frozen cut green beans
1 (16-ounce) can kidney beans, rinsed and drained
4 (14-ounce) cans less-sodium beef broth
¼ cup chopped fresh parsley
½ teaspoon dried thyme
½ teaspoon black pepper
3 garlic cloves, minced, or 1 tablespoon bottled minced garlic
1 bay leaf
1 (14.5-ounce) can diced tomatoes with basil, garlic, and oregano, undrained

1. Heat a large nonstick skillet over medium-high heat. Add sausage; sauté 8 minutes or until lightly browned.
2. Layer potato and next 6 ingredients in a 6-quart electric slow cooker. Top vegetable mixture with sausage. Combine beef broth and next 5 ingredients; pour over sausage mixture. Cover and cook on LOW 10 hours or until vegetables are tender. Discard bay leaf. Stir tomatoes into soup. Yield: 10 servings (serving size: 1½ cups).

CALORIES 160 (8% from fat); FAT 1.4g (sat 0.4g, mono 0g, poly 0.1g); PROTEIN 10.7g; CARB 26.3g; FIBER 4g; CHOL 14mg; IRON 1.4mg; SODIUM 846mg; CALC 66mg

Chock-full of beans, vegetables, and smoky sausage, this recipe takes classic vegetable soup to a new level. The acid in tomatoes can prevent potatoes from getting tender in the slow cooker, so we stirred the tomatoes in at the end.

Thai-Style Pork Stew

Rice vinegar, an essential ingredient in Asian cuisine, is a mild, colorless vinegar made from fermented rice. When shopping for rice vinegar, read the label carefully. Don't confuse it with these other products with similar names: seasoned rice vinegar (which is lightly sweetened and is available in a variety of flavors), rice wine (mirin or sake), and rice wine vinegar (which is made from rice wine and is sweeter than rice vinegar).

Stew:
  2 pounds boneless pork loin, cut into 4 pieces, trimmed
  2 cups (1 x ¼–inch) julienne-cut red bell pepper
  ¼ cup teriyaki sauce
  2 tablespoons rice vinegar or white wine vinegar
  1 teaspoon crushed red pepper
  2 garlic cloves, minced
  ¼ cup creamy peanut butter

Remaining Ingredients:
  6 cups hot cooked basmati rice
  ½ cup chopped green onions
  2 tablespoons chopped dry-roasted peanuts
  8 lime wedges

1. Place pork, bell pepper, and next 4 ingredients in a 4-quart electric slow cooker. Cover and cook on HIGH 1 hour; reduce heat to LOW, and cook 6 hours. Remove pork from cooker, and coarsely chop. Add peanut butter to cooking liquid in cooker; stir well. Stir in pork.

2. Serve stew over rice in individual bowls, and top with onions and peanuts. Serve with lime wedges. Yield: 8 servings (serving size: about ⅓ cup stew, ¾ cup rice, about ½ teaspoon peanuts, and 1 lime wedge).

CALORIES 412 (30% from fat); FAT 13.6g (sat 3.6g, mono 6.2g, poly 2.5g); PROTEIN 28.9g; CARB 42.3g; FIBER 2.1g; CHOL 64mg; IRON 2.9mg; SODIUM 425mg; CALC 37mg

Fragrant basmati rice, peanut butter, and classic Asian flavors meld in this thick stew with Thai flair. As with traditional Thai cuisine, the play between sweet, salty, sour, and spicy creates depth of flavor in this simple recipe that's made even easier in the slow cooker. A squeeze of fresh lime juice is a bright accent to the rich sauce.

Curry Stew with Lamb

Lemongrass adds tartness and lemony fragrance to foods. The herb gets its flavor from an essential oil called citral, which is also found in lemon peel. Lemongrass is available fresh and dried. We used the dried powdered form in this recipe because we were forming a paste (fresh lemongrass was too coarse for this). Look for dried lemongrass in the spice section of your supermarket or in an Asian market.

¼ cup firmly packed fresh basil
    leaves
3 tablespoons chopped
    peeled fresh ginger
3 tablespoons fresh lime juice
1 tablespoon Thai seasoning
2 teaspoons curry powder
1 teaspoon dried lemongrass
    (such as Morton & Bassett)
3 shallots, peeled and halved
1½ pounds boneless leg of
    lamb, trimmed and cut into
    1-inch cubes
2½ cups cubed peeled Yukon
    Gold or red potato
2 tablespoons fish sauce
1 (14.5-ounce) can
    no salt–added diced
    tomatoes, undrained
1 (14-ounce) can light coconut
    milk
Freshly ground black pepper
    (optional)
Basil leaves (optional)

1. Place first 7 ingredients in a food processor; process until a paste forms. Spoon mixture into a 3½- to 4-quart electric slow cooker. Add lamb and next 4 ingredients; stir well. Cover and cook on HIGH 1 hour. Reduce heat to LOW, and cook 7 hours or until lamb is tender. Ladle stew into individual bowls. Sprinkle with pepper, and garnish with basil leaves, if desired. Yield: 6 servings (serving size: 1⅓ cups).

CALORIES 254 (32% from fat); FAT 9g (sat 5g, mono 2.5g, poly 0.4g); PROTEIN 23.8g; CARB 20.8g; FIBER 2.3g; CHOL 65mg; IRON 2.8mg; SODIUM 781mg; CALC 34mg

Lamb curry is a classic dish from northern India. This version includes Thai-inspired ingredients like aromatic lemongrass, sweet coconut milk, and salty fish sauce. These additions provide an excellent backdrop to a bold blend of herbs and spices.

Chicken Brunswick Stew

For this recipe, be sure to use the hot pepper sauce that contains whole peppers packed in vinegar, rather than the red-colored hot sauce. The cured peppers impart their spicy heat to the vinegar, which can be used to season soups, stews, and cooked greens. Bring the bottle to the table when serving this stew, and add more pepper sauce to suit your taste.

5 cups chopped onion
6 (6-ounce) skinless, boneless chicken breast halves
2 (14¾-ounce) cans no salt–added cream-style corn
2 (14.5-ounce) cans no salt–added diced tomatoes, undrained
1 (14-ounce) can fat-free, less-sodium chicken broth
1 (12-ounce) bottle chili sauce
¼ cup butter, cut into small pieces
2 tablespoons Worcestershire sauce
2 tablespoons cider vinegar
2 teaspoons dry mustard
½ teaspoon freshly ground black pepper
½ teaspoon hot pepper sauce
Freshly ground black pepper (optional)

1. Place onion in a 5- to 6-quart electric slow cooker; top with chicken. Add corn and next 9 ingredients, and stir well. Cover and cook on HIGH 1 hour. Reduce heat to LOW, and cook 6 hours or until chicken is tender. Remove chicken; shred with 2 forks, and return to stew. Ladle stew into individual bowls; sprinkle with additional black pepper, if desired. Yield: 9 servings (serving size: 1½ cups).

CALORIES 344 (20% from fat); FAT 7.5g (sat 3.6g, mono 1.7g, poly 0.6g); PROTEIN 30.1g; CARB 39.9g; FIBER 4.3g; CHOL 79mg; IRON 1.8mg; SODIUM 1,335mg; CALC 54mg

Controversy surrounds the folklore of this dish: Some say it was created in Brunswick County, Virginia, in 1828; others insist its origin is Brunswick, Georgia. Virginians usually add butter beans to the mix, which is something Georgians would never do when cooking their barbecue-based stew. Regardless, this spicy stew of chicken, onions, corn, and tomatoes usually has to be tended for hours over a hot stove. This slow-cooker version takes care of itself.

Peasant Stew

Cilantro has a very pungent flavor when it's fresh, but this flavor quickly disappears when cilantro is stirred into hot food. To get the maximum flavor punch, mince and sprinkle the cilantro over a dish just before serving. To mince cilantro, gather several stems into a tight bunch, holding the stems close to the leaves. Use a sharp chef's knife to roughly cut the leaves from the stems. Chop the leaves to the desired size; discard the stems.

1 teaspoon ground cumin
¼ teaspoon salt
¼ teaspoon black pepper
6 chicken thighs (about 1½ pounds), skinned
Cooking spray
1 cup chopped onion
1 (14.5-ounce) can Mexican-style stewed tomatoes with jalapeño peppers and spices, undrained
1 (4.5-ounce) can chopped green chiles, undrained
1 (16-ounce) can pinto beans, rinsed and drained
1 (16-ounce) can kidney beans, rinsed and drained
¼ cup minced fresh cilantro
¼ cup reduced-fat sour cream

1. Combine cumin, salt, and black pepper; sprinkle over chicken. Heat a large skillet over medium-high heat; coat pan with cooking spray. Add chicken to pan; cook 4 to 5 minutes or until browned on all sides.

2. Place chicken in a 5-quart electric slow cooker; stir in onion, tomatoes, and chiles. Cover and cook on HIGH 3 hours. Stir in beans. Cover and cook 1 hour.

3. Ladle 1¼ cups stew into each of 6 soup bowls, and top each with 1 chicken thigh, 2 teaspoons cilantro, and 2 teaspoons sour cream. Yield: 6 servings.

CALORIES 245 (27% from fat); FAT 7.3g (sat 2.3g, mono 2.1g, poly 1.3g); PROTEIN 19.7g; CARB 24g; FIBER 6.6g; CHOL 53mg; IRON 2.7mg; SODIUM 556mg; CALC 101mg

Cumin, green chiles, and Mexican-style tomatoes give this humble stew a spicy kick. Because the chicken thighs are left whole, serve this rustic fare with a knife, fork, and spoon.

sides & desserts

Ratatouille

Here's an easy way to cut bell pepper strips: Slice off the top of the bell pepper, and cut it into quarters. Discard the stem, seeds, and white membranes. Slice each pepper quarter either crosswise or lengthwise into ¼-inch-thick strips.

1 (1-pound) eggplant, peeled and cut into 1-inch chunks (about 3 cups)
1½ teaspoons salt, divided
1 large onion, cut in half lengthwise and sliced (about 2½ cups)
1½ cups green bell pepper strips
1½ cups red bell pepper strips
3 medium zucchini, sliced (about 4 cups)
2 pounds plum tomatoes, cut into ½-inch wedges
3 tablespoons tomato paste
2 tablespoons extravirgin olive oil
¼ teaspoon black pepper
3 garlic cloves, minced
½ cup chopped fresh basil
¼ cup capers
Freshly ground black pepper (optional)

1. Place eggplant in a colander over a sink. Toss with ¼ teaspoon salt. Let stand 30 minutes to drain. Pat dry with paper towels.
2. Layer half each of onion, eggplant, bell pepper strips, zucchini, and tomatoes in a 6-quart electric slow cooker. Combine remaining 1¼ teaspoons salt, tomato paste, oil, black pepper, and garlic. Spoon half of oil mixture over vegetables. Repeat layers, ending with oil mixture.
3. Cover and cook on LOW 6 hours or until vegetables are tender. Stir in chopped basil and capers. Spoon ratatouille into individual bowls; sprinkle with freshly ground black pepper, if desired. Yield: 10 servings (serving size: 1 cup).

CALORIES 76 (38% from fat); FAT 3.2g (sat 0.5g, mono 2.2g, poly 0.5g); PROTEIN 2.6g; CARB 11.4g; FIBER 3.9g; CHOL 0mg; IRON 0.8mg; SODIUM 490mg; CALC 32mg

Ratatouille, pronounced ra-tuh-TOO-ee, *hails from the French region of Provence. Its ingredients—eggplant, onion, bell pepper, zucchini, and tomato—reflect the bounty of that area. Salting the eggplant before adding it to the slow cooker draws excess water out of the porous vegetable, firming the flesh and taking away any bitterness. Serve this side dish warm, at room temperature, or chilled.*

Wild Mushroom Polenta

1 cup yellow cornmeal
1 tablespoon butter
Cooking spray
3 cups boiling water
¼ cup (1 ounce) grated fresh
    Parmesan cheese
2 tablespoons chopped dried
    porcini mushrooms
¾ teaspoon chopped fresh or
    ¼ teaspoon dried thyme
½ teaspoon salt
¼ teaspoon black pepper
Thyme sprigs (optional)

1. Place cornmeal and butter in a 2-quart electric slow cooker coated with cooking spray. Gradually add 3 cups boiling water, stirring constantly with a whisk until well blended. Stir in cheese and next 4 ingredients. Cover and cook on LOW 3 hours or until thick. Stir well before serving. Spoon polenta into individual bowls; garnish with thyme sprigs, if desired. Yield: 6 servings (serving size: ½ cup).

CALORIES 126 (24% from fat); FAT 3.4g (sat 1.8g, mono 0.9g, poly 0.3g); PROTEIN 4.2g; CARB 19.6g; FIBER 2.2g; CHOL 8mg; IRON 1mg; SODIUM 260mg; CALC 40mg

When you're at the store, make sure to buy plain yellow cornmeal and avoid cornmeal mix (which contains flour, leavening, and salt) and self-rising cornmeal (which has leavening and salt). While those products are helpful for baking corn muffins or corn bread, polenta requires the plain version.

Porcini mushrooms lend a strong, earthy, smoky flavor to this savory Italian side dish. Because porcini are some of the most sought-after wild mushrooms, finding the dried variety is often the easiest option. In this dish, the dried mushrooms reconstitute while simmering in the slow cooker with cornmeal and water, saving you a step of preparation. In the store, less flavorful varieties of mushrooms are sometimes substituted for the real thing, so look for porcini's botanical name—Boletus edulis—on the package.

Roasted Sweet Onions

4 medium sweet onions
Cooking spray
3 tablespoons extravirgin olive oil
1½ teaspoons salt
2 teaspoons chopped fresh thyme
2 tablespoons balsamic vinegar
¼ teaspoon freshly ground black pepper

1. Cut each onion into 8 wedges. Place onion in a 6-quart oval electric slow cooker coated with cooking spray; drizzle onion with olive oil. Sprinkle evenly with salt and chopped thyme. Drizzle with balsamic vinegar; sprinkle with pepper.
2. Cover and cook on HIGH 3 to 4 hours or until browned and tender. Yield: 6 servings (serving size: about 5 wedges).

CALORIES 107 (59% from fat); FAT 7g (sat 1g, mono 5.4g, poly 0.6g); PROTEIN 1.4g; CARB 10.2g; FIBER 2.1g; CHOL 0mg; IRON 0.3mg; SODIUM 586mg; CALC 30mg

Use any sweet variety of onion you can find locally for this recipe. Availability depends on the season and location. From late spring to early summer, look for Vidalias from Georgia, Sweet Imperials from California, and Spring Sweets and Texas 1015s from Texas. Walla Wallas from Washington state and Oregon are available from summer through early fall. Look for imported Rio Sweets in autumn. From late winter through early spring, keep an eye out in specialty markets for Oso Sweet onions, a supersweet variety that's imported from South America.

These onions make a great accompaniment to grilled steak, especially since you can tend the grill while the onions cook unattended. For a 1½-pound flank steak, which will serve 6 people, sprinkle steak with ½ teaspoon each of salt and pepper. Place steak on a grill rack or broiler pan coated with cooking spray; grill or broil 6 to 8 minutes on each side or until desired degree of doneness. Cut steak diagonally across the grain into thin slices, and serve with roasted onions. Serve any leftover onions chilled atop a bed of mixed greens with a balsamic vinaigrette and blue cheese.

Root Vegetable Medley

1 pound small red potatoes, quartered

1 pound turnips, peeled and cut into ½-inch cubes

1 pound sweet potatoes, peeled and cut into ½-inch cubes

½ pound celeriac (celery root), peeled and cut into ½-inch cubes

½ pound peeled baby carrots

2 cups thinly sliced fennel bulb

3 tablespoons extravirgin olive oil

2 tablespoons balsamic vinegar

1 teaspoon salt

1 teaspoon black pepper

1 teaspoon fennel seeds

1. Place all ingredients in a 6-quart electric slow cooker, and toss well. Cover and cook on LOW 7 to 8 hours or until vegetables are tender. Yield: 8 servings (serving size: 1 cup).

CALORIES 168 (30% from fat); FAT 5.6g (sat 0.8g, mono 4.1g, poly 0.6g); PROTEIN 3.1g; CARB 27.3g; FIBER 5.1mg; CHOL 0mg; IRON 1.3mg; SODIUM 367mg; CALC 69mg

Though turnips are available year-round, their peak season is from October through February. When they're attached, fresh bright greens and a firm root are the hallmarks of a turnip's freshness. Also look for turnips that feel heavy for their size—these are the young ones. They'll be more delicately flavored and have a better texture than older turnips.

The earthy, mildly sweet flavors in this dish make this an excellent side dish to round out an autumn menu. For an elegant presentation, purchase whole baby carrots with green tops. Trim the greens and peel the carrots before adding them to the cooker. For an everyday meal, prepeeled and prewashed bagged baby carrots will do.

Coconut-Pecan Sweet Potatoes

2 pounds sweet potatoes,
    peeled and cut into 1-inch
    pieces (about 5½ cups)
¼ cup packed brown sugar
2 tablespoons flaked
    sweetened coconut
2 tablespoons chopped
    pecans, toasted
1 tablespoon butter, melted
1 teaspoon vanilla extract
¼ teaspoon ground cinnamon
Cooking spray
½ cup miniature marshmallows

1. Place first 7 ingredients in a 3½-quart electric slow cooker coated with cooking spray; toss well. Cover and cook on LOW 6 to 8 hours or until potatoes are tender. Mash potato mixture.

2. Turn cooker off. Sprinkle marshmallows over potatoes; cover and let stand 5 minutes. Yield: 7 servings (serving size: ½ cup).

CALORIES 155 (21% from fat); FAT 3.7g (sat 1.6g, mono 1.3g, poly 0.6g); PROTEIN 1.7g; CARB 29.6g; FIBER 2.8g; CHOL 4mg; IRON 1mg; SODIUM 48mg; CALC 37mg

There are many types of coconut available on the market: sweetened or unsweetened; shredded or flaked; canned, frozen, or dried. Flaked sweetened coconut is the most widely used and is a useful staple ingredient to keep on hand. Look for it in bags or cans on the baking aisle. An unopened bag of flaked sweetened coconut can keep in the pantry for six months; once opened, it needs to be refrigerated and can be kept for up to one month.

This sweet-potato classic is a favorite at Thanksgiving, and that's exactly when your oven is in high demand. This slow-cooker version not only saves oven space, but it also stays nice and warm in the cooker while you finish cooking the other dishes.

Steamed Brown Bread with Currants and Walnuts

Molasses, a product of the sugar-refining process, is the liquid left behind after sugar crystals have been extracted from boiled sugarcane juice. Several different versions are available. The light variety comes from the first boiling and is usually used to top pancakes. The second boiling creates dark molasses, which has a denser, more assertive flavor; it's most commonly used in gingerbread and barbecue sauces. Avoid blackstrap molasses, which comes from the third boiling; though popular in health-food circles due to its slightly higher mineral content, it's very bitter.

½ cup all-purpose flour
½ cup whole wheat flour
½ cup yellow cornmeal
¾ teaspoon ground cinnamon
½ teaspoon baking soda
½ teaspoon salt
1 cup low-fat buttermilk
⅓ cup molasses
½ cup dried currants
2 tablespoons chopped walnuts
Cooking spray

1. Lightly spoon flours into dry measuring cups; level with a knife. Combine flours and next 4 ingredients in a large bowl, and make a well in center of mixture. Combine buttermilk and molasses, and stir well. Add to flour mixture, stirring just until moistened. Fold in currants and walnuts.
2. Spoon mixture into a 1½-quart round casserole dish coated with cooking spray. Cover with aluminum foil coated with cooking spray; secure foil with a rubber band. Place dish in a 6-quart electric slow cooker; add enough hot water to cooker to come halfway up sides of dish. Cover and cook on HIGH 2½ hours or until a wooden pick inserted in center comes out clean.
3. Remove dish from cooker using oven mitts. Let bread cool, covered, in dish on a wire rack 5 minutes. Remove bread from dish, and let cool completely on wire rack. Yield: 8 servings (serving size: 1 wedge).

CALORIES 170 (13% from fat); FAT 2.4g (sat 0.5g, mono 0.3g, poly 1g); PROTEIN 4.4g; CARB 34.5g; FIBER 2.3g; CHOL 0g; IRON 1.9mg; SODIUM 252mg; CALC 82mg

Bread probably isn't what you think of as typical slow-cooker fare, but this method of steaming the bread in the cooker helps the batter cook evenly and makes for a moist texture. Serve this bread as a side to complete a meal or as a light breakfast with coffee. You can substitute sweetened dried cranberries for the currants, if desired.

Walnut-Stuffed Apples

¼ cup coarsely chopped walnuts

3 tablespoons dried currants

2½ tablespoons brown sugar

¾ teaspoon ground cinnamon, divided

4 Granny Smith apples, cored

1 cup packed brown sugar

¾ cup apple cider

1. Combine first 3 ingredients in a small bowl; stir in ¼ teaspoon cinnamon. Peel top third of each apple; place apples in a 5-quart electric slow cooker. Spoon walnut mixture evenly into cavities of apples.

2. Combine remaining ½ teaspoon cinnamon, 1 cup brown sugar, and apple cider in a small bowl. Pour over apples. Cover and cook on LOW 2 hours and 45 minutes. Remove apples with a slotted spoon. Place 1 apple on each of 4 dessert plates, and spoon ¼ cup cooking liquid over each serving. Yield: 4 servings.

CALORIES 310 (14% from fat); FAT 4.9g (sat 0.5g, mono 0.7g, poly 3.6g); PROTEIN 1.9g; CARB 70g; FIBER 3.8g; CHOL 0mg; IRON 1.6mg; SODIUM 23mg; CALC 60mg

Dried currants come from the Zante grape, a tiny grape that's intensely sweet. Although Zante grapes can be found fresh in specialty markets when they're in season, they are most often dried to make currants, which are commonly used in baked goods. Dried currants are not to be confused with fresh currants—berries that are related to the gooseberry. The berries called currants are eaten fresh or used to make preserves, syrups, and liqueurs.

Tart Granny Smith apples are drenched in a syrupy brown sugar glaze. Currants are a delectable addition to the classic caramelized nut topping. Serve these "baked" apples warm with low-fat frozen yogurt, if desired.

Saucy Apples 'n' Pears

3 Gala apples (about 1½ pounds), peeled and sliced
3 Anjou or Bartlett pears (about 1½ pounds), peeled and sliced
1 tablespoon fresh lemon juice
½ cup packed dark brown sugar
½ cup pure maple syrup
¼ cup butter, melted
¼ cup chopped pecans
¼ cup raisins
½ teaspoon ground cinnamon
2 tablespoons water
1 tablespoon cornstarch

1. Place apple, pear, and lemon juice in a 4½-quart electric slow cooker; toss gently.
2. Combine brown sugar, syrup, and butter. Spoon sugar mixture over fruit. Stir in pecans, raisins, and cinnamon. Cover and cook on LOW 5½ hours.
3. Combine water and cornstarch in a small bowl; stir until well blended. Stir cornstarch mixture into fruit mixture. Cover and cook 20 minutes or until slightly thickened; stir well. Yield: 4½ cups (serving size: about ⅓ cup).

CALORIES 171 (28% from fat); FAT 5.3g (sat 2.4g, mono 1.9g, poly 0.7g); PROTEIN 0.6g; CARB 32.9g; FIBER 2.5g; CHOL 9mg; IRON 0.6mg; SODIUM 30mg; CALC 27mg

Unlike flour, cornstarch will thicken a sauce without turning it opaque. It's ideal in fruit toppings because it won't mask the color and texture of the fruit. Whisking it with a little cold water before adding it to the other ingredients prevents lumps in the sauce. Make sure to turn off the slow cooker after the sauce has thickened. If cooked too long, cornstarch loses its thickening power, causing the sauce to separate and become thin.

Enhance the bounty of late fall's best pick of apples and pears with the soothing flavors of pure maple syrup, pecans, and cinnamon. Your whole house will be filled with warming aromas as the apples and pears simmer in the slow cooker. Serve this warm fruit topping with ice cream or pound cake or over pancakes.

Caramel Pie

1 (14-ounce) can fat-free
   sweetened condensed milk
1 (6-ounce) reduced-fat
   graham cracker crust
1 (8-ounce) container frozen
   reduced-calorie whipped
   topping, thawed
1 (1.4-ounce) milk chocolate–
   crisp butter toffee candy bar,
   coarsely chopped

1. Pour milk into a 2-cup glass measure; cover with foil. Place in a 3- to 4-quart electric slow cooker. Add very hot water to cooker to reach level of milk in measure. Cover and cook on LOW 9 hours (milk should be caramel colored). Stir well with a whisk.

2. Pour caramelized milk into crust; cool. Spread whipped topping over pie; sprinkle with chopped candy bar. Yield: 8 servings (serving size: 1 wedge).

CALORIES 321 (23% from fat); FAT 8.3g (sat 4.6g, mono 0.5g, poly 0.1g); PROTEIN 5g; CARB 57.2g; FIBER 0.1g; CHOL 9mg; IRON 0.4mg; SODIUM 153mg; CALC 134mg

Sweetened condensed milk has been a staple pantry item for well over 100 years. It's used in a variety of desserts—from candies and cakes to pies and ice cream. When cooked for a period of time, sweetened condensed milk is transformed into a gooey caramel that forms the filling of this pie. Using a slow cooker is a safe alternative to the old-fashioned method of cooking the milk in the can—a procedure that has been proven dangerous.

This luscious pie requires only four simple ingredients. Keep them on hand and you'll always have the makings for a winning dessert.

all about
Slow Cookers

A slow cooker is a busy cook's best friend. Follow our tips and techniques to ensure a wholesome, delicious meal every time you use this convenient appliance.

Slow-Cooking Benefits

In addition to allowing you to make meals ahead, your slow cooker offers these benefits:

• **Easy cleanup** You have only one container to wash and no container if you use the new heavy-duty plastic liners.

• **Environmentally friendly** A slow cooker uses less electricity than the cooktop or oven. There's no extra heat escaping, so the kitchen stays cool.

• **Requires little attention** You don't have to stand over a hot stove or watch the clock. The slow cooker works best when it's left alone to slowly simmer food. Generally, a little extra cooking time won't ruin a dish.

• **Adaptable** Most traditional recipes that call for long, slow, gentle cooking in a Dutch oven are adaptable to the slow cooker. Some of your family's favorite recipes can be ready as soon as you walk through the door at the end of a busy day.

• **Economical** Tough, less expensive cuts of meat are transformed into tender, moist, and richly flavored dishes when cooked in the slow cooker.

• **Healthier** The tougher cuts of meat are also the leanest, and seldom do you add fat when cooking meat and poultry in the slow cooker. During the long simmering time, fat will rise to the top of the cooking liquid and can be removed before serving.

• **Portable and versatile** The slow cooker can be located any place where there's an electrical outlet. It's especially useful when entertaining or when counter space is limited. You can prepare hot drinks and appetizers in the slow cooker and place the cooker where your guests will gather. Just make sure to use the LOW setting.

Best Cuts of Meat for the Slow Cooker

Type of Meat (3 ounces cooked)	Calories	Fat (sat)
chuck or rump roast	206	13.1g (sat 4.9g)
tip roast	199	11.3g (sat 4.3g)
lean beef stew meat	201	9.6g (sat 3.6g)
lean Boston butt roast	197	12.2g (sat 4.4g)
lamb stew meat	158	6.2g (sat 2.2g)

New Versus Old

Does it matter if your slow cooker is a hand-me-down classic or a new shiny model with gadgets to boot? Either will work, but the age of your cooker may affect the cook time.

Some new slow cookers cook at a slightly hotter temperature than older models. If using a newer model, check for doneness at the lower end of the time range.

Older models, on the other hand, probably need to go to the longer end of the time range. To make sure your older slow cooker is getting hot enough to cook foods safely and thoroughly, the Food Safety Information Society recommends this test.

1. Fill your slow cooker between half and two-thirds full with water.
2. Cover and cook on LOW 8 hours.
3. Remove the lid, and immediately check the temperature with a thermometer. The temperature should be 185°. A lower temperature indicates that your cooker does not heat food fast enough or get it hot enough for food safety. Invest in a new slow cooker. (A higher temperature, on the other hand, indicates that your food would be overcooked after 8 hours on LOW. In this case, check food for doneness a little early.)

Visit foodsafetyline.org for additional information.

Purchasing

If you're in the market for a new slow cooker, here are some of the options available today—from the most basic to high-tech models.

Basic Options

• *Size:* Slow cookers come in round and oval shapes, as well as in a variety of sizes—from 16 ounces to 7 quarts, with half sizes in between. Choose the size that fits your lifestyle best. If you have a large family or entertain often, you may want to opt for a larger size. Or you may want to purchase a second slow cooker of a different size.

• *Removable inserts:* Slow cookers with removable inserts are easier to clean than one-piece units. Depending on the manufacturer, the insert may be dishwasher safe.

• *External timers:* This is one option that you purchase separately from your slow cooker. This clever external device is similar in concept to the timers you use to turn lights on and off while you're out of town. Simply plug the external slow-cooker timer into the wall outlet, and then plug your cooker into the timer. It allows you to set your cooking time; when that time has expired, the timer will automatically switch the cooker to warm. It's a handy option if you don't own a slow cooker that allows you to preset the time.

Specialty Products on the Market

If you demand more from your slow cooker, consider one of these models.

• *Hamilton Beach 5-Quart Double Dish Slow Cooker:* This model offers two ways to cook—prepare one dish in the five-quart stoneware bowl, or use the divided nonstick Double Dish to cook two recipes at the same time.

• *Rival 6-Quart Versaware Slow Cooker:* The stoneware pot functions as a slow cooker in a removable electric base. The pot can also be used on the stovetop or in the oven. Afterward, use it to store leftovers in the refrigerator or freezer.

• *Rival 5.5-Quart Recipe Smart-Pot:* This one offers programmable settings for temperature and cooking time and stays warm for up to four hours after the cooking cycle is complete. Use your own recipe, or choose from more than 200 preprogrammed recipes digitally stored in the electronic display.

• *Cuisinart 6.5-Quart Slow Cooker:* A sleek, stainless steel exterior houses a generously sized removable pot. Nice features include an automatic "warm" setting that is used after cooking is complete, retractable electrical cord storage, and a cooking rack that accommodates ramekins or other bakeware.

Easy Cleanup

• Allow the slow cooker insert to cool completely before washing it. Cold water poured over a hot insert can cause cracking.

• Never immerse a slow cooker unit in water. Simply unplug it and wipe it clean with a cloth.

• Buy clear, heavy-duty plastic liners made to fit 3- to 6½-quart oval and round slow cookers. Just fit the plastic liner inside your slow cooker before adding the recipe ingredients. Simply serve the meal directly from the cooker. Once the cooker has cooled, just toss the plastic liner.

Food Facts

• *Dried beans* may take longer to tenderize if salt, sugar, or an acidic ingredient (such as tomatoes) is added at the beginning of the cook time. For best results, add any of these ingredients after beans have cooked until tender. For more information on beans, see page 141.

• *Dairy and seafood* tend to break down when cooked for extended periods. Unless otherwise instructed, add dairy products during the last 15 minutes; add seafood within the last hour.

• *Whole herbs and spices,* such as cinnamon sticks and bay leaves, do well in the slow cooker because they release flavor throughout the long cooking time. Be sure to remove them, however, before serving food. Fresh herbs should be added at the end to add fresh flavor and color to the finished dish.

• *Vegetables, especially root vegetables like carrots, onions, and potatoes,* often cook slower than meats and, therefore, need direct contact with the bottom and sides of the cooker. Place vegetables under meats in the slow cooker unless otherwise instructed.

• *Pasta and rice* can be tricky when prepared in a slow cooker. Follow the recipe directions for the best time to add the pasta or rice to the cooker. Always use long-grain converted (parboiled) rice for slow-cooker recipes.

Essential Secrets to Slow-Cooker Success

A quick review of the following guidelines will guarantee healthy and delicious slow-cooker meals any night of the week.

Size Matters

Use the slow-cooker size specified by the recipe to ensure proper levels of food, thorough cooking, and safe temperatures. If you do try a different-sized cooker than specified, make sure it's still between half and two-thirds full for food safety. Be aware, however, that cooking time may vary accordingly (for example, if using a larger slow cooker, the cook time may be less; if using a smaller cooker, your dish may need more time).

Know Your Slow Cooker

If your slow cooker gets hotter than average, as some newer models do, you'll need to adjust the cook time accordingly. For more information on slow-cooker temperature variation, see New Versus Old on page 136.

Keep a Lid on It

Removing the cooker's lid during cooking releases a great deal of heat, so resist the urge to lift the lid and peek. Each time you remove the lid when not required, you'll need to increase the cooking time by 20 to 30 minutes.

Trimming the Fat

Slow cooking is a moist-heat cooking method and thus requires little fat. Trim excess fat and skin from meats and poultry for low-fat cooking and visual appeal.

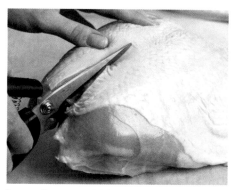

Large Pieces of Meat

Cut pieces of meat or poultry larger than 2 to 3 pounds in half—these smaller portions will ensure thorough cooking.

Uniform Pieces

When cutting meat or vegetables into chunks, make sure the pieces are a uniform size. This ensures the pieces will cook evenly. Otherwise, some may be overdone or underdone.

Browning Meat

For visual appeal and extra flavor, brown meat and poultry in a skillet and drain off any fat before adding the meat to the cooker. If you use cooking spray, remove the hot pan from heat before spraying it with cooking spray.

Layering Ingredients

Layer ingredients, especially vegetables, as the recipe directs. Don't stir the ingredients unless a recipe specifically calls for it. For more information, see Food Facts on page 137.

Adding Liquid

Use only the amount of liquid specified in a recipe. While amounts may seem low, more juices cook out of the ingredients, and there's less evaporation than in traditional cooking methods.

Time Conversions

Remember that 1 hour on HIGH equals approximately 2 hours on LOW. A bonus to cooking on LOW is that recipes can generally cook a little longer than the recipe states without becoming overdone.

Thickening

During the last 20 to 30 minutes, thicken juices or make gravy by removing the lid and cooking on HIGH. A slurry of flour (or cornstarch) and liquid added to the cooker will thicken juices even more.

Slow-Cooker Safety

Slow cooking is a safe method for preparing food if you follow the standard procedures. Here's what the U.S. Department of Agriculture (USDA) recommends.

• *Keep ingredients refrigerated until ready to use.* If you prepare ingredients in advance, keep meats and vegetables separate. Because slow cookers don't heat food as quickly as conventional appliances, it's especially important not to allow perishable ingredients to sit out at room temperature, which would let bacteria grow.

• *Whenever possible, cook all meats on HIGH for the first hour.* This creates steam and gets the food cooking quicker. The strategy is aimed at quickly bringing cooking temperatures up to levels needed to prevent the growth of bacteria. (We sometimes omit this step in recipes that brown the meat first. Browning increases the initial temperature of ingredients.) If you won't be home to reduce the temperature, it is okay to cook for the entire time on LOW, according to the USDA. In this case, substitute 2 extra hours on LOW for the 1 hour on HIGH.

• *Thaw frozen meats completely before cooking;* don't cook meats from a frozen or partially frozen state. Thaw meats in the microwave, if necessary.

• *Don't cook whole poultry (such as a whole turkey breast or roasting hen) or a whole roast in the slow cooker* because they can't heat up fast enough, and some parts will be in the temperature range that is ideal for bacterial growth. Cut any roast or poultry piece over 2 or 3 pounds in half.

• *Don't reheat leftovers in the slow cooker.* They can't heat up fast enough, so there's a chance of bacterial contamination. Instead, use the microwave or stovetop.

• *Always fill a slow cooker at least half full and no more than two-thirds full* in order for food to cook properly. The starting food level is what's important; it's okay if food cooks down.

• *If the power goes out while you're away, throw away food in the slow cooker.* If you're at home when the power goes out, uncooked food can finish cooking on a gas stove; completely cooked food will remain safe in the cooker for two hours.

• *Use an instant-read thermometer to check the internal temperature of large pieces of meat.* Here are the safe temperatures to reach:
  Beef: 145° to 170°
  Lamb: 145° to 170°
  Pork: 160° to 170°
  Poultry: at least 170°

• *Always use an oven mitt or cloth and lift the lid away from you* when removing it from the slow cooker. This allows any accumulated steam to escape safely.

Basic Accompaniments

The tasty juices that accumulate in your cooker are often so flavorful that you won't want to let a drop go to waste. The following basic recipes, prepared on the stovetop or in the oven, are ideal for sopping up extra sauce or gravy.

Pasta

Dried pasta takes about 20 minutes to cook on the stovetop, including bringing the water to a boil. Pasta yield depends on type and shape, so the serving size may vary for an 8-ounce package.

12 cups water
8 ounces dried pasta

1. Fill a 4-quart pot with 12 cups water. Cover and bring to a boil over high heat (omit any salt or fat specified by package directions).
2. Uncover and add pasta. Stir. Return to a boil, and start the timer.
3. Check for a doneness a few minutes before the time indicated on package directions. (Pasta cooked al dente should offer resistance to the bite but have no trace of brittleness.)

4. Drain in a large colander over a sink. Serve with a pasta fork or tongs. Yield: 8 servings (serving size: ½ cup).

CALORIES 103 (3% from fat); FAT 0.4g (sat 0.1g, mono 0g, poly 0g); PROTEIN 3.9g; CARB 21.1g; FIBER 0.9g; CHOL 0mg; IRON 0.9mg; SODIUM 1mg; CALC 5mg

Couscous

This tiny pasta, made from semolina (durum wheat) flour, is native to the Middle East. It's so simple to prepare that it may become your favorite accompaniment to slow-cooker fare. Try it with Apricot and Lamb Tagine, page 54.

2 cups water
1 (10-ounce) box couscous

1. Bring 2 cups water to a boil in a saucepan (omit any salt or fat specified by package directions). Stir in couscous. Remove pan from heat; cover and let stand 5 minutes. Fluff with a fork before serving. Yield: 9 servings (serving size: ½ cup).
Note: If you're making your couscous ahead, there's no need to boil the water. Just add the same amount of water to the couscous; cover and chill overnight or until the water is absorbed.

CALORIES 118 (2% from fat); FAT 0.2g (sat 0g, mono 0g, poly 0.1g); PROTEIN 4g; CARB 24.4g; FIBER 1.6g; CHOL 0mg; IRON 0.3mg; SODIUM 3mg; CALC 8mg

Rice

Served on the side, rice is better cooked on the stovetop or in a rice cooker. (You will find some recipes that instruct you to add converted rice to the slow cooker.)

1 cup brown rice
2¼ cups water

1. Combine rice and water in a saucepan (omit any salt or fat specified by package directions).
2. Bring to a boil, reduce heat, and cook, covered, 30 minutes or until water is absorbed (do not lift lid during cooking). Fluff rice with a fork before serving. Yield: 8 servings (serving size: ½ cup).
Note: For a quicker option, use boil-in-bag rice. It cooks in 10 minutes. You'll need 2 (3.4-ounce) bags to yield 8 (½-cup) servings of cooked rice.

CALORIES 86 (7% from fat); FAT 0.6g (sat 0.1g, mono 0.2g, poly 0.2g); PROTEIN 1.8g; CARB 18.1g; FIBER 0.8g; CHOL 0mg; IRON 0.4mg; SODIUM 1mg; CALC 8mg

Mashed Potatoes

Chicken broth and milk make these mashed potatoes rich; sour cream gives them tang. Try these with Pork Chops and Gravy, page 26. Or serve Saucy Italian-Style Chicken Thighs, page 62, over these potatoes as an alternative to pasta or rice.

   3 pounds cubed peeled baking
      potato
   ½ cup 2% reduced-fat milk
   ½ cup fat-free, less-sodium chicken
      broth
   3 tablespoons reduced-fat sour
      cream
   1 teaspoon salt
   ½ teaspoon black pepper

1. Place potato in a saucepan, and cover with water. Bring to a boil. Reduce heat; simmer 15 minutes or until tender.
2. Drain and return potato to pan. Add milk and broth, and mash to desired consistency. Cook 2 minutes or until thoroughly heated, stirring constantly. Stir in sour cream, salt, and pepper. Yield: 12 servings (serving size: ½ cup).

CALORIES 84 (9% from fat); FAT 0.8g (sat 0.4g, mono 0.1g, poly 0g); PROTEIN 3.3g; CARB 15.4g; FIBER 2g; CHOL 3mg; IRON 0.7mg; SODIUM 228mg; CALC 25mg

Corn Bread

Corn bread, a terrific side to hoppin' John, gets a crisp crust when you preheat the oil in the pan.

1¾ cups yellow cornmeal
   ¼ teaspoon baking powder
   ¼ teaspoon baking soda
   ¼ teaspoon salt
   1 cup 1% low-fat buttermilk
   1 cup water
   1 large egg
   1 large egg white
Cooking spray
   3 tablespoons vegetable oil

1. Preheat oven to 375°.
2. Combine first 8 ingredients in a large bowl; stir well. Coat a 9-inch cast-iron skillet with cooking spray; add oil, and place in oven 5 minutes. Remove from oven; stir oil into batter. Pour batter into pan. Bake at 375° for 35 minutes or until golden. Yield: 9 servings (serving size: 1 wedge).

CALORIES 161 (32% from fat); FAT 5.8g (sat 1.1g, mono 1.4g, poly 2.9g); PROTEIN 4.4g; CARB 22.4g; FIBER 2g; CHOL 25mg; IRON 1.2mg; SODIUM 157mg; CALC 42mg

Cooking Dried Beans

Beans make a hearty addition to slow-cooker dishes and are a valuable source of fiber, antioxidants, and protein. If you're making a dish where beans are featured but are not the main ingredient, chances are you'll need beans that are already cooked.

Cooking your own dried beans allows you to keep the amount of sodium to a minimum. (When we call for cooked beans, the nutritional analysis reflects beans cooked without salt or fat.) A 1-pound bag (about 2 cups) of dried beans will yield 5½ to 6½ cups of cooked beans. Before cooking dried beans, you'll need to soak them.

For quick-soaking, add 6 to 8 cups of water to 1 pound of dried beans, and bring to a boil in a Dutch oven. Cover and cook 2 minutes; remove from heat, and let stand 1 hour. Rinse and drain, and then cook according to package directions.

For overnight soaking, add 6 cups of water to 1 pound of dried beans. Let stand 8 hours at room temperature. Cook according to package directions.

If substituting canned beans for cooked dried beans, 1 (15-ounce) can of beans equals 1¾ cups of drained beans. Rinsing canned beans gets rid of the thick liquid in the can and reduces the sodium by 40 percent.

Subject Index

Recipe Index

143